Abdelkader Benali was born in Ighazzazen, Morocco, in 1975 and has lived in the Netherlands since 1979. He won the Best Literary Debut Prize of 1996 in Holland and was shortlisted for the Dutch equivalent of the Booker Prize, the Libris Literatuur Prize. He is currently studying history at Leiden University. *Wedding by the Sea* is his first novel.

Wedding by the Sea

ABDELKADER BENALI

Translated by
Susan Massotty

PHŒNIX

A PHOENIX PAPERBACK

First published by Uitgeverij Vassallucci, Amsterdam, 1996

First published in Great Britain by Phoenix House in 1999
This paperback edition published in 2000 by Phoenix,
an imprint of Orion Books Ltd,
Orion House, 5 Upper St Martin's Lane,
London WC2H 9EA

The publishers would like to acknowledge the financial support of
the Foundation for the Production and Translation of Dutch Literature
which has helped to make this translation possible.

A CIP catalogue record for this book
is available from the British Library.

ISBN: 0 75380 953 2

Typeset at The Spartan Press Ltd,
Lymington, Hants.
Printed in Great Britain by
The Guernsey Press Co. Ltd, Guernsey, C.I.

That's the way we do things

Lamarat Minar didn't live in Iwojen. Unlike Chalid, the man with the brown teeth and reversed rearview mirror, the driver of the white Mercedes cab who knew, by virtue of his profession, every hill, hogback ridge and gully in the entire Iwojen region, the man who knew the source of the buzzing sound, the drone coming that afternoon from every agave, the insistent hum of the cicadas: Chalid, the taxi driver who cruised the roads, never dared to marry and thought lawn chairs were for wimps. Somehow he was even able to conjure up a picture of Lamarat Minar, the son of the son of the father from that village by the sea, the kid who hadn't been back to Iwojen since he was ten. Chalid's ability to conjure him up only goes to show that the people of Iwojen, not counting the dead, suffer from a neurotic self-imposed need to remember. Another thing that Chalid – or 'Bucket of Bolts', as the lame, the blind and the deaf, holed up in various cafés and courtyards, liked to call him as they washed and ritually removed the toe-jam from the feet they couldn't move, see or hear (but could smell) – had remembered was the birth of this very same Minar. In Iwojen, in a village, in a square house, just as the grandmother was making *mtsimeni* for her lazy daughter-in-law. Chalid could have told the story of the birth to anyone who asked and was able to spare the ten half-dirhams for the ride to the border town of F. He could easily have told the story of the umbilical cord and the old lady's prompt response – the truthful lie that had passed into collective memory – since it showed that the boy was linked in some small way to the region, like a big fat rutabaga that oddly enough only got fatter the further it got from the root and perversely went on growing in a landscape that was otherwise as dry as a bone.

The twenty-year-old Lamarat Minar, the boy who had got into the cab, had been born somewhere in the Iwojen region. Wherever you go in Iwojen you run into villages, donkey shit and urban sprawl. If you're coming to Iwojen from the sea, the first thing you see is the village of Mira Mora, clustered around a spring. A little further on, before you go to the pine forest, there's Tintin and to the east of the hills, Jefella. On the other side of the forest you can feast your eyes on Mossarat, Ezeboch and Verster. Then there's the border town of F., home to waiting taxis and Africans, which serves as the gateway to the Spanish crown colony of Melilliar – the city where it's so much cheaper to buy soap, margarine and Tide detergent, items smuggled by the thousands under dresses and burnooses, the only city in Iwojen in which there are more women than men, lots more. And if you're going further or happen to come from there, there's Al Homey, a boom-town favoured by returning emigrants and chiefly char-acterized by unchecked growth. And here the women are greatly outnumbered by the men. (Most of the men in Al Homey are looking for a wife; you can almost hear them shouting, 'A wife, a wife, my wisdom for a wife!') It was in this town that Lamarat's father, as behoves a model emigrant, had ordered a house to be built, a house with five pillars and water pipes, though the pipes were soon clogged with cockroaches and crumbling mortar. This was also the town in which he promised, in exchange for

2

the house, that his brother could marry his daughter, who was left in the lurch on the day of the wedding. All of which took place in the village that was further away from Al Homey than any other village in Iwojen, a village named . . . Touarirt.

Touarirt, a handful of houses by the sea. There, between the chicken coops and the sheep pens, between 'The Wind of San Antonio' and 'Our House', in an abode called 'The Wolf's Den', Lamarat Minar had been born, or so he had been told. Lamarat the Superstitious ('Why do you call me that?'), Lamarat the Lunatic ('Is this a joke or what?'), Lamarat the Limitless, the Furtive, the Spiteful, the Teeth-Gnasher, the Pretender, the Grown Wrong (just how many nicknames can a person take?), who had come to stay in his native village for several days to celebrate an unforgettable wedding, had been born one sunny Saturday morning to a mother and father who, before they were married, had lived up the hill from one another, in the village of Touarirt on the Mediterranean Sea, at a time that one of them thought of as ages ago and the other as only yesterday, but in any case far, far, far away from Thalidomide babies and birth control.

The two families on the hillside lived practically cheek by jowl. In one house there was a boy and in another a girl – that's asking for trouble – who years later, in time-honoured custom, would become the father and mother of one and the same person. The two houses owned by the families of the future father and mother of Lamarat Minar were separated by a burgeoning row of cactuses dotted with red, yellow, orange and green prickly pears, growing on a patch of land conveniently located between the two cube-shaped houses. Surrounding them on all sides were the terraced fields of grain worked by the father's family.

'A farmer doesn't *always* have a hard life,' Lamarat

Minar's grandfather had once told his father when he was teaching him the fine art of dirt farming. 'You just have to do what our forefathers have been doing for hundreds of years, what my father taught me and what I'm teaching you: take some seed, sow it, then hope and pray that Sidi Rabbi will do the rest.' The father blessed this educational homily with a short but sweet, all-purpose *inshallah*. And strangely enough, it was on that very same cactus-studded plot, between the fields of grain, between the daily repetitions of *inshallah*, that love sprung up between Lamarat Minar's father and the mother-with-the-raven-hair.

Their affection blossomed along with the prickly pears littering the higgledy-pick-them-peel-them-eat-them-piggledy plot of land, where they attempted to see each other as often as they could in the sometimes long and sometimes short period between dusk and the last mumbled prayers of their two fathers and one mother, who were busy looking the other way (Mecca lay in a different direction).

But beware, danger is lurking everywhere, in every nook and cranny. Don't let other people see into your hearts, young lovers, or they might stab them with their rusty knives!

The boy and girl were in love. But since they weren't crazy about the knives of busybodies, they made sure no one would be able to observe their feverish trysts, always agreeing to meet when everyone in Touarirt was either praying or eating dinner or doing both at the same time, although the latter required a physical agility that was rarely, if ever, displayed in Touarirt and surroundings.

Anyway, they were desperately in love, there between the prickly pears which looked like they'd been pinned to the tall cactuses, and the dried-up clumps of shit – the cactus field doubled as a toilet for the two families –

4

which looked like they'd been baked on the earth. It's enough to make you stand up and cry, 'That's a pretty shaky start to a steady relationship!' And then sit down and reply, 'You're telling me, with every move you make you have to keep one eye on your feet, so you won't step in your own doo-doo or in somebody else's, and another eye on the horizon to make sure nobody has seen you.' Not an easy task for your average shitkicker.

No matter how careful they were, one of them occasionally stepped on something they shouldn't. 'Never mind, sweetheart,' the mother would coo when a dark-brown smear had caked her slipper. 'It's supposed to bring luck. Or something like that.' And back and forth the words would flow, filled with the sugar and honey you need to catch each other's flies. The father promised her, in line with local custom, almost everything his body had to offer: his heart, liver, lungs, spleen, intestines, stomach, brains, tongue, etc., everything but his dick – that would come later. Enough organs to make a haggis were being offered at bargain rates, and all to convince the mother that his surrender had been total. And the mother? What did she do? She listened and nodded and thought it was all too wonderful for words. Sometimes his promises would make her mouth water, would make her stomach rumble so much that she'd suddenly dash through the cactus field as if someone or something was about to plant a knife in her heart; she'd zigzag around the shit, sneak some bread and raw onions from the kitchen and race back, carefully manoeuvring her way through the cactus field again, where she and the father would look deeply into each other's eyes as they ate.

According to those so-called romantic films they show in Melilliar, I ought to be making my move now, the father would think. But what move? I mean, what moves are there?

5

Since the young couple had other people to consider, their trysts were never long. When dusk had unmistakably fallen, they would tear themselves away from each other and off they would go, back home to wash, eat, pray and get up again without fail for a new day.

To Lamarat's future father a new day meant toiling away at the various parcels of land owned by his family, which were scattered throughout the village. Because the terrain was hilly and the narrow paths couldn't accommodate plough animals, Touarirt relied on terracing. This required a great deal of backbreaking work. The father, Machiler Minar, of the father, Terut Minar, had several small terraces with loose but usually blazing hot soil on which he grew grapes. The good man also managed to eke out a few onions, potatoes and carrots on some land he owned a couple of miles away, down in Iwojen's green valley, near the so-called town of San Antonio – 'Got its name from some Spaniard who used to live there, a long time ago,' the father's father was able to report. From time to time Machiler would sell his produce in the crown colony of Melilliar, ten or so miles to the north. He'd ride there on horseback with wicker baskets full of fruit and vegetables. The Minars made a decent living and they were happy. So far so good.

Also happy were the people in the house on the other side of the cactus field, the one in which Lamarat's future mother lived. The occupants of this dwelling, four square walls made out of mud, horse manure and bamboo, were the only people in Touarirt, perhaps the only people in the entire region, who didn't have to lower themselves to such activities as sowing, ploughing, harvesting and bringing baskets of grapes and onions to Melilliar. The family in that house, a mother and four daughters, of whom it was said – though I never saw them and Bucket of Bolts Chalid

6

didn't know the girls either, but it must be true since everybody says so – that one was more beautiful than the other and that they knew it too, lived off the generosity of their father, who was far, far away in France, where he had some kind of job in the coal mines near Strasbourg. From time to time they'd receive a money order worth a sizeable number of francs and an occasional picture of father on a bicycle, father on a motorbike, father in a Mercedes Benz and father in a hostel (broom in hand, peering at the camera). Because of the great riches that had fallen their way, the four girls who lived in the house and shared a tiny bedroom, came to possess virtues that were not held in high esteem in Touarirt. The four nymphs, Jamina (the oldest), Minora, Zuleikha and Batita (the youngest) were no strangers – and no one thought it the least bit strange – to conceit, laziness and pride. 'We can afford to do nothing, and if you can afford to do nothing, why should you do anything but talk about doing nothing,' they said in defence of their privileged position. And they giggled and tossed their hair at the thought of their circular logic, which was part and parcel of another bit of circular logic, in which one of the sisters, say Batita, would stand up, untie her raven hair, go over to the mirror and repeat, while running her fingertips over her body, 'Look at me, I'm beautiful. My shoulders are so soft; my eyes so honest; my lips so sweet; my arms so round; my ears: so tiny, so different, so much better! I must be the fairest in the land, the fairest in the whole wide world. Tell me honestly, sisters, don't you think I'm just too beautiful to be walking around this earth?' And the other sisters would nod and nod and nod until it was time for the next one to take the brush and stroke her neurotic self-esteem.

If only you could hear yourselves talk, you silly girls, while you're having your affair with the mirror, while you're admiring the olive oil on your hair. But do they

7

listen to me? No, of course not. You see, I never met the girls. I heard this story in some café or other, and it's gone from mouth to mouth and from ear to ear so many times that for all I know, Touarirt never even existed.

Thanks to the money that kept flowing in from the north and the mother's inability to calculate how many half-dirhams there were in a franc, the girls were able to buy all kinds of baubles and beads that the local competition could only dream of owning. And to treat themselves to frilly dresses and jet-black scarves from 'town'.

But the affluent life extended to more than gewgaws and clothes. Fish and meat were in plentiful supply (so why the mother always gave the father bread and onions is still a mystery to me – perhaps it was a romantic tradition in that region?), and a daily diet of such delicacies led to bulges, or perhaps we should call them opulent curves, around their hips, arms, buttocks and cheeks. The mother and the girls looked healthier than they actually were because despite their surplus physical energy they did nothing, absolutely nothing. (For example, before she was married, Jamina – the girl who would later, under unusual circumstances and with the help of her mother-in-law's sharp incisors, bear her firstborn child, Lamarat Minar – had never baked bread, never boiled an egg, never taken a sickle to a field of grain, never even dished up a bowl of fish or meat from the stewpot; in fact, the only time she had shown the slightest interest in food distribution had been back in the days of the throbbing heart, when in an overflow of love she had supplied her suitor with bread and onions, but since she had been in the grip of forces beyond her control, that doesn't count.)

In all fairness and truth it can be concluded that the girls were overfed, smug and stuck-up. A second point,

8

not to be overlooked, is that despite these obvious character flaws, they were the only girls in the village worth talking to because you never got tired of looking at them. So the boys in the village paid them a steady stream of attention that looked as if it would never dry up – in fact, at a certain moment the mother had been promised so many organs that she could have started an organ bank. The girls would sit out by the front door, fussing with each other's hair like a pack of monkeys, and this would inevitably cause a stir, so that there was a great coming and going of young men from the surrounding countryside, who kept asking the mother when the oldest was finally going to settle down, all of which sent the mother, who was no great beauty, into a frenzy: 'Wait'll your father gets here, then you'll see how *he* takes care of things, he'll go after those girl-crazy goons with a hammer, he'll rip their eyes right out of their sockets, one by one, until it hurts so much they won't know whether they're dead or alive.'

'Really, Mother, you know how hard it is for boys, always having to sleep together in one room, hot sultry nights . . .'

You might say, to throw a charitable light on things, that the reason Lamarat's mother and her sisters believed from childhood that the earth revolved around their dazzling selves was simply because they'd never run into anyone more beautiful.

But the truth is . . . it wasn't until the boys of Touarirt (which these days is totally bereft of both beautiful girls and backward boys) had gone one by one or in groups to the cinema in Melilliar and seen the bare navels and legs of American, French and Indian beauties for the first time in their lives that they figured out that the girls were really quite ordinary. The more they went to the city, the less entranced they were by the sisters, whom they saw as they came down Sugar Mountain, traipsing around the court-yard, combing their hair with mirrors clutched in their left hands or waddling around in utter boredom.

'You know what I think,' one of the villagers said to the future father as they worked their way one fateful day down Sugar Mountain's terraces, walking along the narrow twisting path that led past Sidi Gallush cemetery.

'No, what?' asked the father timidly, his thoughts straying to the girl he had known since the day he was born, the girl who had become even more beautiful in that barren landscape of dirt clods and dung while he was having more and more trouble with his sweaty feet and fingers, which invariably got nicked when he cut the grain because he couldn't seem to get the hang of the sickle.

'What I think,' the villager continued, 'is that those four girls down there aren't what they're cracked up to be. All that prancing around with mirrors and beads. You call that style? They lie around all day like pigs, and who knows if they'll ever be *halal*. Nah, they don't do a thing for me. Give me the tits of that French chick any day. Did you see 'em busting out of her dress? Humongous knock-ers, incredible! It made me so hot I came all over my hand without even realizing it.'

At this point an intellectual might interrupt to say, 'If I've grasped the situation correctly, the arrival of that Kleenex box they called a cinema signified the end of the mythical beauty of the four girls and the beginning of their *de facto* demystification.' And that perceptive person would be right, because after that no one was stupid enough to give the girls a second glance.

Except for one frustrated soul: the future father. The future father despised the other boys in the village, who had started earning money by doing a little cigarette smuggling here and a low-level construction job there, which meant that they no longer had to resort to goats but could slake their thirst for pussypussypussy in Melilliar. Such wickedness, the father would think – Jamina will soon be mine. And he realized that he had to keep pursuing her, had to develop a more convincing wink, had to hum more of those dopey cowboy songs from the films whenever she passed by on the way to visit relatives in some godforsaken hole . . .

If only he could keep it up, if only he could pray more often and think of other women less. Such a combination of virtues was bound to lead to success.

And success quickly followed. The future mother and her sisters couldn't help noticing that their popularity, not to mention the wet dreams they had once sparked off in the boys, had plunged to unknown depths, in fact might even have hit rock bottom, so that they needed to embark on a new course before people started calling them old maids, though they had no intention of letting things get to that point. . . Luckily the future mother had swiftly realized that the yokel up the hill, 'Elephant Ears', as the four sisters teasingly called him, had an eye, or rather two eyes, on her. She began to flirt back. To the total dismay of the three sisters. That he wanted *her*, okay, that was easy to understand, but what they couldn't understand was why she wanted a relationship with *him*.

'Have you gone nuts?' said one. 'That hayseed, that Dumbo? Why not wait, sister dear? You can do better.'

'Besides,' the youngest teased her, 'you're not really the type for a wedding, for a man, especially a man like that who'll take your earrings and treat them like some hook he can hang his hat on.'

'She's right,' the next one added, 'Use your head, sister. He'll work you to death, like a donkey. Or worse, treat you like a slimy frog, ha ha ha, a slimy frog that won't know which way to turn!'

And so it went – in the living room, in the bedroom,

even in the kitchen (a place they normally didn't frequent), and at night they hounded her with well-intentioned warnings. 'He'll hurt you.' 'He's a monster.' 'He'll eat you alive, you idiot.' They poked fun at their sister and poked even more fun at him, the guy up the hill, the guy with the elephant ears and gnarled onion hands.

Stung as she was by her sisters' remarks, Jamina didn't budge an inch. To pester and scold them, she said, '*La, illaha, illalah,* watch out, because he who laughs at others calls a curse down on himself.' And then she lavished as much attention as she could on the father, responding to his attempts to woo her with a playful look here, a sharp retort there.

'Don't whistle so loudly, neighbour, your lips might get stuck in a pucker,' was her idea of a snappy come-on as she strolled past his terrace, on the way to nowhere, and watched him thrash the grain. Does that mean she wants to marry me? the father wondered, and he was so shocked by his premature conclusion that he cut himself again on the sickle.

Despite the sisterly witticisms, less than a year later, after he had polished off a hundred and fifty onions and a hundred and fifty hunks of bread and she had scraped his doo-doo off her right slipper fifteen times, he popped the question. 'Enough kisses, enough chitchat and enough dates,' the father said to the mother. 'Will you marry me or won't you? I can't live by love and your eyes alone.' And the mother said yes.

Not long afterwards, actually that same evening, late in the summer, on one of the hottest days of the year, the young man strode over to his father. He was lying in the left-hand corner of the courtyard, where there was a slight breeze, with his head in his wife's lap, scanning the sky for shooting stars. The future father didn't know what to say, so he talked a mile a minute, only managing to squeeze in his news between reports of rising grain prices and overfertilization: 'I'd really like . . . I mean, with your permission. . . . as soon as possible . . . with the girl next door . . . no, not up the hill . . . down . . . because I . . . do you know what I'm saying or don't you, Mother . . . are you listening . . . it's time to start making babies, Father, and all that kind of stuff . . .'

At the word 'babies' his father stood up. He stood up the way he usually did when it was time for dinner or a new day or another cigarette; in short, he stood up like he always did and said, 'Go ahead, that's the way we do things around here.'

Nobody in Touarirt dared to believe it. 'What! Dumbo's gonna marry *her*, the raven?' But a couple of months later the future father-in-law flew over with a new pair of shoes for the groom, and the diva of Touarirt was duly married to her 'Elephant Ears'.

The wedding feast, organized by the groom's family, included *mtsimeni* (flaky pancakes), *tekrischt* (offal bubbling in boiling water and oil) and the father's friends, who wondered how he was going to manage with 'Miss Lah-di-dah'. Luckily (especially for Lamarat), the father was sure he knew best: 'Who wants a fairytale princess who can't bake bread?' And he went ahead and married a woman who dreamed of becoming a film star.

By the way, the three sisters, who had been looking forward to the wedding and especially to the wedding night – 'How big will the bloodstain be, what colour, and what if he can't get it up?' – weren't on hand for the red-letter day because all three of them had died, within a few weeks of each other, before the nuptials could take place. The youngest, thirteen-year-old Batita, was the first to go: bitten by a snake on her virginal Achilles heel the very first time her mother sent her, over her wailing protests, to fetch water at the spring. The second sister, seventeen-year-old Zuleikha, exchanged the temporal for the unknown a week later: she cut her hand on a nail, a nail that had sat in the wall for years, inconspicuous and shy, waiting for her fat fingers and warm blood. 'Ha, gotcha, you snooty bitch,' the nail said. Zuleikha was the only one to hear it. The nail was rusty, and she got lockjaw. The third sister, Minora, simply up and died at the ripe young age of nineteen. She passed away quietly, her blanket clutched to her plump body, on a weekday afternoon three weeks after the second sister had died, at an hour when the other residents of Iwojen were snoring and siesta-ing.

After so much grief – the girls were mourned by all of Touarirt since they might not have been the most beautiful girls in the world, but they were 'our' most beautiful girls in the world – a wedding was a welcome diversion. It was time to whoop it up, to paint the town red. They didn't miss a single spot – especially not the big red spot on the spanking-white sheet. The sisters would have been proud.

After the wedding the mother moved up the hill, to her in-laws' house, where she entered an entirely different world. Within days she'd made the staggering discovery (at least to her) that her youth had been spent in the lap of luxury. Suddenly, on the morning after the wedding night, she found the bed empty. He's gone to the market, she reasoned. Then the mother-in-law screamed at her that as the newest member of her husband's household, she was expected to *do* something. 'Like what?' the mother asked. She crawled out of bed, put on her nicest clothes and reported to her mother-in-law. It seemed that what she was expected to do was to make *mtsimeni*, knead dough, fetch water and even tend the goats from time to time – and that was only the beginning.

This rude lifting of the veil – the reality her dearly departed sisters had warned her about (she sometimes thought she could see their words floating above the house) – embittered the mother so much that a seed of discontentment was sown. This seed, born of sheer will-power, was to be a baby that would deliver her from the toil and sweat of daily chores. I can't go on like this, she thought, and in those hot honeymoon weeks she would spread her legs – she had got the hang of it fairly quickly – even wider for her husband so that he could come more deeply and deposit even more of his seed, thereby upping her chances of producing a labour-saving child. Sidi Rabbi willing, she would add in a burst of pragmatism. And so it didn't take long for the miracle to happen: exactly eight months to the day, eight-pound Lamarat (a name he was given later) was born.

On the day of the birth they each had their own concerns. The father was in Deutschland, the grandfather was threshing grain, the grandmother was looking for more bandages to staunch the flow, and the brand-new mother was trying to hide her disappointment. The baby had been born a month too soon so she was going to miss a whole month of extra attention: *Woe betide him who refuses a pregnant woman anything – the baby will be born with a handicap.* But since there was more than one road to unemployment, she decided to devote herself to the child, or at any rate pretend to devote herself to the child – to rock it constantly, to nurse it until her nipples fell off, to do whatever it took as long as she didn't have to make *mtsimeni* and fetch water. Fortunately for the mother (as well as the child), she wasn't forced to take such drastic measures, because six months later – with a baby boy in her arms and another little goldbricker in her tummy (a girl: that too had been part of her calculations) – she left for Holland, where she found herself enjoying the relative quiet of a house with wood floors and an antenna on the roof. At last! she thought. Nobody ordering me to make *mtsimeni*, no more goats and no more bleating in-laws. And so Ollanda, Sesame Seed Land – which the mother-in-law stubbornly referred to as Deutschland – was also more or less her salvation.

Mosa was the father's younger brother. And also the person Lamarat had been sent to find, the person who had created such an uproar in the village by the sea, the uncle who had failed to wave goodbye to Lamarat when he and his mother had left for 'the West' because he was busy ogling the girls by the spring. Girls in slippers and pyjama-like trousers with bells in their hair, scarves around their hair knots and enough talk for ten. Mosa was crazy about the girls, though not one of them was crazy about Mosa. Still, all that looking makes you hot and heat needs an outlet, so thanks to those powerful physical reactions and the stories he'd heard, he found his way at a tender age to Melilliar, the city of shalom, women and pour-me-another-glass-of-Ricard. He was not quite twelve when he first did something that he wouldn't understand completely until five years later.

The arrival of cinemas and buses and the razing of the Jewish synagogue had sparked off a new service industry in Melilliar. The city was inundated with individuals eager to make use of it, including Mosa who was a regular customer long before he knew exactly what he was doing. What he did know was that the activity to which he was devoting himself with such zeal and nervous greed was not allowed. It was bad, cursed, a no-no, forbidden fruit, not for children but for grown-ups; in short, it was *haram*. It was *haram* and you knew it was *haram* because . . .

well, because people didn't talk about it and if they did, it was in such low whispers that you couldn't help but hear, in which case you found out where you could do it and how much it cost you to do it and how often you could do it, but especially, and this was said in an even lower voice, that it would be better for you not to do it at all.

Still, it was *haram* for both big boys and little boys.

'But I'm a man, dammit, and I know damn well what I'm doing with those women so why shouldn't I! Besides, who says women are forbidden before marriage? Huh, don't make me laugh.'

Mosa, the son of Machiler, the man who came back from every trip to town and told his father how many he'd twisted around which little finger, the man from Touarirt, that picturesque village by the sea, had become hooked on women at an early age. He wasn't the least bit tongue-tied around women of easy virtue. He was hopelessly in love with the girls with the hennaed hair, the queens of the streets. Nobody knew what he did in Melilliar – but then you never knew what other people did in Melilliar. So nobody knew that when Mosa went off with a supply of green beans, maize and grapes, he would tie his horse to a tree in the market-place and, after selling his produce, transfer his earnings from their usual place in his right pocket to his left pocket and quickly make his way, hooray, to that female paradise, Lolita's Bar.

Nobody knew what he did at Lolita's either, but it must have been something on the order of: women who've put on eye shadow and sultry, seductive voices, men dancing to the sounds of tambours and kemenjas, and all that for free, runs in nylons, eyes focused on those runs and the little hairs peeping out from them, tables that rock, hands that shake, and at last one of those babes coming over and sitting down beside him, patting his hand and wiping the sweat from his brow – at first Mosa didn't say anything, not a word, just watched – but when he headed back to Touarirt and a friend of his popped up from behind the onion fields and cactuses and asked, 'Where've you been, off for a little fuckie-fuck again?' he knew exactly how to make that one gesture (one sign in the hand is worth three in the bush) that would say it all: he would nod, and that would mean something like, Yeah, hot diggity, I got laid! And they would immediately think: Aha, he's been to the 'Hush-Hush House' again.

No, no, let's switch over to her head. After all, she has a speaking part. (A woman's voice determines her street value.) Her name? Any name you want: Nightshade, Rosemary, Pound of Liver, Nefertiti or that old standby, Concubine. 'Okay,' she says, 'so you're not very big, but a little pot soon gets hot, how much money have you got, little man?' Then she gets up, leaving the rest of the hip-swivellers and drink-clutchers in the bar and slips out in the afternoon light to her usual room in Lolita's Hotel. Peeling off first one run and then the other, she jams the bills into a money clip and says, 'Go lie down. Hey, what's wrong, little one, cat got your tongue? You washed your balls this morning, didn't you? You do keep up your daily ablutions, don't you, kid?'

And Mosa nods, yes of course, yes here, yes no, yes always, yes what am I supposed to do next, yes what are you going to do next. Am I lying the right way move over a bit up and down hey what's that why can't I touch you how come you won't let me kiss you on the lips what do you mean unwritten rule help I'm flying it's better than milking cows froth and sticker albums back and forth up and around shit it's coming oh no not so fast and that was the end of the story. What'd she done to Mosa? He couldn't tell you exactly. A lot, it seemed to Mosa. Not much, she always thought.

*

18

What if the father had known about Mosa's trips to Melilliar? Would he still have said to his little one, 'Well, son, Mosa, gosa, losa is your uncle, zippidy-do-da, your one and only uncle, zippidy-ay, and he's going to teach you how to swim in our nice warm sea'? Would he have dared to marry off his daughter, as she looked on from her crib, would he have dared to put her and her unsullied reputation in Mosa's hands? We don't know. But the father talked about his brother and tickled his son until he collapsed into giggles.

Mosa, who tickled himself, was about five years older than Lamarat. He grew up surrounded by the ghost of his big brother, Lamarat's father. He couldn't stick a spade in the ground, dig up an onion or herd a donkey to the spring in San Antonio without someone looming up out of the houses and hills and asking, 'How are things going with your brother in the north and when are you going to follow in his footsteps?' Hmm, you're thinking, why not simply shrug your shoulders, say, 'He's fine, everything's okay', and continue stoically on your way. But how can you avoid so much attention when everybody is always asking, 'When will you be heading north?' After all, he had a brother there, someone who could help him with money, a job, the trip over. And not just to any old country in Europe – not Spain where those dirty Franco dogs spit on you, not France, not Deutschland, but the best country in the whole wide world: Ollanda! Only a fool would pass up a chance like that. 'But', he replied when his best friends stopped for a chat, 'what have they got over there that we haven't got here? We're not exactly starving to death in Iwojen. Or are we? Look at the grapevines, they're flourishing, all the crops are, the onions, the carrots, the eggplants and soon yumyum there'll be corn on the cob. And don't forget that prickly pears grow here for free – I've got a whole field of them behind my house!'

'You're a babbling idiot,' they said, 'and also blind as a bat. Listen, Touarirt is dying.' And they pointed to their surroundings, in a sweeping gesture that went from one hilltop to another with the sun in between (you're such con men, Mosa thought, not unkindly, if you clapped your hands, you'd clap the sun shut). And to the fields that were drying up at an alarming rate – they were right about that. And to the grapevines, which weren't producing enough grapes. 'Everybody's into growing these days. But whether you live in Melilliar or Al Homey, you can count on one thing: you won't see a penny of it.' Is that true, Mosa wondered to himself, or am I starting to think like them? 'Well, honey, let me tell you, the money's up there where your brother is, no matter how you look at it, no matter what kind of work he has to do to earn it.' Every time he ran into someone, it was always the same story, and you'd have to be crazy not to admit that they were right, even if the streets up north weren't really paved with gold.

It was in this period that Mosa began contemplating marriage to his brother's daughter, Rebekka, who was far away in Sesame Seed City playing *Red Rover, Red Rover Let Someone Come Over* with her girlfriends.

Around the world in eighty moves

The boy, unaware of his mother's motives for bringing him into the world or Mosa's for marrying Rebekka, had always dreamed of life in Iwojen. Of how good things would have been if his family had stayed there, living out their lives between the damp clay and the starry firmament, eye to eye with God, with the thousands of gods around which life revolves, or so he mused; and when he climbed into the cab his heart ached even more because he realized – a person does a lot of brooding – that he'd missed not only a life of beauty, but also one of riches, fame and honour.

What this young man had no way of knowing when he set off in search of his uncle, leaving behind his father, mother, sister and various relatives in that fig-tree-and-cactus village, was what he would have become if he and his mother had stayed in Iwojen, in a region surrounded on three sides by water. Lamarat Minar: ten fingers, ten toes and a scar underneath his eyebrow, a reminder of the time he'd been playing around with a knife; this scarred boy, who for some reason had seated himself in the front beside the driver, would undoubtedly have become a Parcheesi player: roll the dice and go around the world in eighty moves. That is, if he'd stayed in Iwojen, if he'd gradually learned the game, if he'd got to know people, if he'd trailed along with them to the cafés after school – he would have eventually mastered the art of Parcheesi, or Ludo as it's known in some parts of the world. But rats, it wasn't meant to be: his mother had snatched him up and put him on the plane. And because of that chance transfer, he had missed out on a glorious and fortune-filled future in Iwojen.

Actually, his future as a Parcheesi player had been clear from birth. His grandmother, who had helped him into the world, had noticed it (the taste of blood still clinging to her lips) the moment she first clapped eyes on him: this was going to be the most perfect Parcheesi player Iwojen had ever produced. The premature baby had survived the difficult birth and got through the first two weeks without a sign of decline. So the grandmother said to the mother, who had been hoping for a slight frailty, 'The child's had a lot of luck, two dice full of luck; hopefully that diabolical luck will never desert him.'

Perhaps, Grandma, perhaps. But then you should have wept louder and tugged harder on your son's shirt-sleeve when he decided to take your little bundle of joy away. In that case the child – Lamarat Minar was his name – would now be the right age (provided the story is told correctly), to be making his first triumphal march around the tables and chairs in the region's many cafés, so that the grandmother could be swelling with pride at his inherited luck and grit. In those establishments – a fancy name for a greasy spoon with a 12 x 15 Real Madrid poster tacked to the wall and a floor littered with sunflower seeds; in those cubby-holes where they sat around all day drinking mint tea – that's where Lamarat Minar would have made a name for himself: in one of the many little boxes on the hillside, no different to the others you find along the asphalt road twisting its way through Iwojen like a garden hose through a dried-up cornfield. A winding road that the taxi driver had traversed roughly forty-thousand times in the thirteen years he had been on the job.

The taxi driver was what you'd call an old pro. Bucket of Bolts Chalid had seen the inside of nearly every café along the asphalt road at least once; he'd either picked up passengers there or played an occasional game of Parcheesi when business was slack.

In the cafés in Iwojen, the cardboard Parcheesi boards were covered by a sheet of glass to protect them from wet and greasy fingers. If the story had gone as it was supposed to, Lamarat would have been destined to walk into those cafés, greet people, pull up a chair, fix his eyes on the pawns – 'Do you want red, yellow, blue or black, Minar?' – and roll the dice: to pass the time, but mostly to win, almost a sign of depravity in some parts of the country. Alas, when the boy sitting beside the taxi driver moved away, a great Mephistopheles was lost to the world.

He sat uneasily in his seat, because he'd been given enough orders to fill his heart and ears with dread. No, he was never going to be an ace Parcheesi player, never going to hit major-league Parcheesi – it just wasn't in the dice.

Can fathers be held responsible? Could you take the biological father to court for the wilful obstruction of his progeny's future? Did he act with malice aforethought? Does the father also like to play games? After all, it was Lamarat's father who nipped that potential ambition, that brilliant career, in the bud. A father, a *padre*. Yep, you guessed it – a big hulk of a guy, crude, balding, unshaved *and* with big ears; exactly the type that caused such mayhem in Chicago during Prohibition. All that was needed to complete the picture was a gun in his pocket and a hat on his bald head. And to think that it was this non-pistol-packing brute who had torn the child in early infancy away from Iwojen's sphere of influence and taken him to the outside world. To *Ollanda*.

That the father would leave for 'the West' was already a foregone conclusion. Everyone knew he was going – the taxi drivers in the region knew it, the Parcheesi players in the cafés knew it, even the unborn babes in their mothers' wombs knew it. They heard it via their mothers, who would gather by the spring in groups of four, five, six, seven to ten, along with the leading lights of their lives: the donkeys, tethered in a clump, chewing and listening to the women babble as they took turns filling their empty *bombats*, two-gallon olive-oil jugs, with the gushing water.

'Who'd you say was thinking of going away?'

'*Leh, leh, leh*, no no no, he's really going!'

'*Ai*, Dumbo, Jamina's husband!'

'If your Dumbo's going, Jamina, I have only one thing to say: may Sidi Rabbi guide him and may only good things come his way.'

'But if he really is going, Jamina, my child, then why oh why?'

'Hey, my husband's not like yours! Mine's a real doer, a raw-onion-and-bread kind of guy – he's not interested in words, but in *things*.'

Since the pregnant women in Iwojen were in the delightful habit of meeting each other several times a day by the spring to talk, chat, gab, blab and yak – and to do so much of it so often with so many other women – all that idle talk was bound to trickle down, along with the gurgling of the spring, into the deepest recesses of the mother's womb. So before Lamarat had even had his first glimpse of the world, that world was as clear as a well: life consists of cramming as many two-gallon jugs of spring water as you can into donkey baskets. After that, deciding whether to stay or to go. And, of no less importance, wondering what the father should wear on the day he goes away, since 'The clothes

24

you leave in are an indication of how well you'll do when you come back.' Clever, and true. Only too true. As it happens, the father, who on the day of his departure was already a prospective father – his child, curled inside its mother, was listening to the women rattle on about 'Elephant Ears' and what'll we cook to-night – went off dressed in his weekday worst, as if he'd stood up one fateful day in Iwojen's onion fields and thought: Hmm, why don't I take a little stroll to Deutschland?

'But you can't do that,' his father had screamed at him. 'You look like a tramp. What'll the women of Touarirt think?'

'What does it matter what I have on, what does it matter whether you smoke Marlboro instead of Casa Sport? It's time for me to go, and that's that,' the future father had replied (all the while thinking, You old fart – just as disrespectfully as Lamarat did years later when his father sent him out to find his missing uncle).

The father left Touarirt, leaving behind everything but the contents of one small suitcase. His wife, spilling over with new-found joy and morning sickness, had been heartlessly abandoned, had been left barefoot and pregnant, or so they might say in more affluent areas. He didn't even kiss her goodbye, but left her standing in the kitchen with her mother-in-law. He walked out of Touarirt and over Sugar Mountain to the winding asphalt road, where he flagged down a taxi. 'Where're you going?' asked the taxi driver. 'To Deutschland to earn a living,' he said.

Over there in 'the West' he had the time of his life. 'Back in those days,' the father would say if you casually pumped him for information, 'we were in great demand with the white girls because, except for a handful of Italians and Spaniards, there were hardly any of us.' And it was true. Alone and all on his own in Holland, the father thought of himself as a perennial bachelor even though he believed he'd only be there for a short while. (Back when he still believed in fairytales, he said to the mother, 'Honey, it's like this. I'll be gone for six months, eight at the outside. Just till I've earned enough to make sure I'll never have to shovel another clod of dirt again. Then I'll buy a café and a couple of Parcheesi boards and we'll be all set. From then on in, all I have to do is make tea and sell a little *kif*.' After which he kissed the mother and made passionate love to her to atone for his boasting because, as Lamarat also knew, things were bound to turn out differently.)

He stayed a year, two years, ten years and finally he'd spent thirty years announcing at every meal that this year would be the last. 'I'm going back, for good. Away from this land of pork and rotten bananas.'

Lamarat – big nose and a tendency to exaggerate – and his sister Rebekka – matured in Holland, ohlala, and with her *madre's* dark hair – were obliged, during the nightly round-table monologues of *Wewe* the Mastodon (eventually everything and everybody becomes extinct), to adopt the well-known classic attitude of put up or shut up. The TV was always on (a bomb here, a hijacking there and one day a huge earthquake in Mexico – collective reaction of the sports writers in Europe and elsewhere: World Cup Football in danger) and if you didn't agree with the people on the TV you were free to scream and shout and swear at them all you wanted. That's what TV was for. But as for Pa: pay attention and snap to attention. 'I'm your father, the, you know, alpha and omega. I brought you over here and if all goes well, I'll take you back there some day.' Every once in a while Lamarat couldn't help grinning at his father's act, which wasn't shown on TV but was reserved exclusively for a select group of sister, brother and sometimes mother. 'What do you mean go back, *Wewe*, back when, *Baba*, and while we're at it, where to, baboon?'

'Cut it out, this is no laughing matter. You'll have to go back to your fatherland eventually, because any day now . . . oh, if you only knew . . .'

'What do you mean any day now? What don't I know, *Wewe*?'

'Oh, you don't understand a thing, you spoilt brat: the third world war, boom, everything wiped out in one blow and everybody eating out of dustbins, then it'll really be over and out! One of these days World War III's gonna break out here, if it hasn't broken out already. You heard me, World War III.' The father said it so often and with so much satisfaction that it almost looked like he believed it. 'And when the plague hits Holland, where are you gonna go? I bet you won't be so eager to stay here then.' War as the proverbial stick and his fruitful prick as the means of legitimizing his authority. 'You'll do as I tell you, or else all hell is gonna break loose in Holland and the rest of Europe. You kids have no say in the matter because you haven't accomplished a thing. Who created you? Go ahead, tell me, and don't you dare say "Allah."'

Try to imagine, go ahead and give it a whirl, that you dared to respond to his raunchy little routine: 'Hey, Pa, what do you mean we haven't accomplished anything?'

'Incredible!' he'd shout. 'Standing up to your own father, incredible, incredible. Sidi Rabbi, oh Sidi Rabbi, why have you given me such wicked brats?'

How many times had they sat around the table while the father, his left hand resting on the mother's plump knee and his right hand clutching a lamb cutlet, would be struck over and over again at so much cheek on the part of his children? For example, Lamarat would cut the fat off his lamb chop and the father would see it. Which was a disaster because he'd start again on the dustbins and bananas. 'When I was your age I was happy if I found a banana peel in a dustbin in Melilliar. Gimme that!' he'd say, and he'd wrench the fat from Lamarat's fingers and cram it in his mouth. It was true: he left home because he wanted to eat more, see more, do more. 'Holland is *haram*, if you know what I mean. You won't believe what they gave us to eat when I first came here. Pork! Every evening they stuffed us full of pork. I had pork coming out my ears!'

Perhaps we should note, just to set the record straight, that his very first pork chop wasn't served to him in Holland, but in Belgium. Before he'd even finished unpacking in the hostel near Hoboken they had plonked a pork chop on his plate. Years later, and I mean six times five fingers, he'd still be smacking his lips and describing that meat in juicy detail. 'That pork chop might have been forbidden, but it went down all right.' He liked to recount the meal, bite by bite, especially when he was feeling peckish and had ordered the mother to start peeling the potatoes.

Anyway, he didn't stay in Belgium for long; he hated working in the mines – 'If I'd wanted to get my hands dirty I could've stayed at home' – and fled to Holland. After a stint in Venlo (Tourist Office), Culemborg (Marynen Refrigerators), Utrecht (Reaal Insurance) and Amsterdam (Apropos Wallpaper Plant), where he was employed to give the nooks and crannies a good going-over with a mop and broom, he finally wound up in Sesame Seed City. It was the mid-seventies and Lamarat had just been born, though he only realized that he had a child and had actually become a father when the taxi driver transporting him over Iwojen's asphalt road asked him how the baby was doing. 'What baby, where?' the father asked in bewilderment.

'Your little boy, the one who was born, uh, let's see, it must have been about three months ago.'

Ha, thought the father, so the kid's already here. I forgot all about it. But if it's a boy she hadn't done bad at all, my Jamina, not bad at all, and he asked what they'd named the baby.

'Name? He hasn't got a name yet. Everybody's been waiting for you to name him.'

'So what's your name?' the father asked the taxi driver.

'Me? I'm Chalid Ben Balla, but my father was called Moktar, and his father was called Lamarat,' the cabby replied.

The father asked him to stop at the dirt road down to the village and thanked him. 'I'll name him Lamarat,' he said in parting, 'after the father of the father of a taxi driver.' And that's just what he did.

Soon after his arrival in the village he got fed up with hearing the women go on and on about bitten-off umbilical cords, drooling babies and deserted mosques. He packed his bags and left, but not before announcing a few minutes before his departure, that he would send for his wife and child as soon as he could arrange for them to come to Sesame Seed City. His bachelor existence couldn't last forever, he told himself. Every good joke has an ending. And he bid farewell to the cafés, the discos and the beer.

Right about then, the shipyard that employed him to clean the nooks and crannies of their oil tankers went bankrupt. 'It's time we turned to Islam,' he said to whoever was willing to listen, and he started going to the mosque (it was a period of massive lay-offs and droves of people were doing the same). Coming home from the communal prayer hall, he would drink tea and break bread with his wife and tickle his steadily growing and prone-to-falling-out-of-his-bunk-bed son from head to toe, and that was that. Until the beginning of the eighties, when he heard – in the mosque, in the cafés (which he went to every once in a while for a quick game of Parcheesi), in the butcher shops and even in his sleep – 'Al Homey, that's the place to be right now; the land's cheap and there's plenty of cement and construction workers. Buy land, buy land, buy land, do you know what I'm saying or don't you?'

The father had a little money stashed away in a foreign bank. He'd glance at the statements, rip them up and burn them. 'Good riddance to bad rubbish,' his wife would snap, and he'd count the days until enough interest had accumulated to enable him to start building a house.

Along with the falls from the bunk bed, the ebb and flow of men to the prayer halls, the shredded bank statements, the bags of money piling up on the credit side – 'Interest is *haram, haram* is interest but don't worry, Lord, as penance I'll fast longer, no, pray more, no, have my house built on five pillars to atone for that diabolical interest, or would that be a tribute to the interest?' – along with all these things the father began to warm to the idea of marrying off his daughter Rebekka to his little brother, who spent all his time doing nothing and loafing around Touarirt.

It was Chalid, the taxi driver, who would later say to Mosa on the day that Lamarat got into the cab to look for him, 'Where're you going? I hear you've decided to head out for Europe after all, you crazy guy. At any rate, the girl you're marrying will be your ticket to Ollanda. This country might be *hek-o-hek*, so-so, but you couldn't pay me to go to a country where the women boss you around and walk all over you:

Marry her, marry her,
A daughter of Deutschland,
Give her a chance,
To break her feet on your back,

a country where they stop you if you drive through a red light and treat you like an idiot . . . I wouldn't even do it if you gave me a bucket of gold, my friend, do you know what I'm saying or don't you?'

'She's okay,' Mosa had said to Chalid. 'She's family.'

'Go to Deutschland or wherever it is you're going, do you know what I'm saying or don't you, but even if she's an angel and the best of the best your family has to offer, once she's back on her own turf she'll change into a devil. To that kind of girl, kinship and family ties don't mean a thing; she'll treat you like a slave.'

Words like that hit hard. They made you wonder about the motives of your friends. So, Chalid, the uncle thought, you're one of those, and the rest of them too. First you wish me luck and kiss me on the cheek and forehead, but once you're through slobbering, your true mentality comes to the fore: you're nothing but a bunch of hypocrites luring innocent people into a trap. And it was true – no one envied him. Right after he announced, a year before his departure, that he too had finally decided to go, his friends said in exasperation, 'How can you be so stupid – if you're going to Ollanda, you ought to be single. At least that way they'll leave you alone. Free as a bird, and all that stuff. But no, not you. You want to be happily married, you say. That's what *you* think. But watch your step: that girl's gonna be on your tail and you won't be able to get that fat brother of yours off your back. They'll box you in so tight you won't be able to breathe . . . We've told you a thousand times, but you probably weren't listening: either go by yourself or stay here in

Iwojen where you've got it good. By the way, now that we're on the subject, grapes are going for a good price in Melilliar and the crops are looking good . . .'

Curtain up, curtain down

Ironically, on the day that Mosa fled from his wedding, the crops were far from flourishing. The sun had scorched every plant that had stuck its costly head above the ground, every last one of them, down to the tiniest raisin-sized grape. But Mosa didn't notice the heat that day, or the financial ruin being visited on Touarirt and the surrounding regions. He wanted to be somewhere else, far away from the hoopla going on around him. He decided to make himself scarce so he crept out of the bridal chamber, crossed over the cactus field and dried-up creek beds and left the village, heading for a place, the *only* place, that he could go to without having people fire a lot of questions at him.

Everyone in Al Homey and Iwojen knew where Mosa had gone. Everyone, that is, except the family of the bride and groom. Mosa the Humper, the Hellcat, the Front Man, the Life of the Party, the Leper, had gone to his favourite cuddle-me spot to say goodbye to his favourite cuddle-me lady.

'Chatischa, my darling Chatischa,' said Mosa the Romantic, 'you know I'm going far and will be long gone, but I'll never forget you.' Shit, thought Mosa the Hypocrite, with a lump in his throat – for some reason his words sounded strange to him. What seems to be happening, he mused, is that my fucking heart has run away with my voice. I don't even know what I'm saying anymore. And what am I doing here in this bar when I should be at my wedding? You asshole, you're supposed to be getting married and you're with a whore. 'Come on,' Mosa said to her, 'let's do it one last time.'

And Lamarat Minar, who happened to be passing by and saw them come out, was thrown into a state of confusion (strange women had a strange effect on him), and he thought what I too am thinking, namely that this story should actually be taking place on a stage. One chock-full of puppets. That would suit me (and my father) better – I could keep my story simple. Boy puppets and girl puppets, each with its own colour and rigid, well-defined symbolism. At least Lamarat and I, not to mention the mother (a bit) and the sister (a lot), would know where we stand. If you could think of this as a puppet show, you'd find it easier to see what's really going on and realize that the usual puppet symbolism is totally lacking in this story. However, there is no puppet theatre – the boy's father never gave him any toys (except once: a cake for his birthday, which was supposed to be eaten; food is a very important toy).

So in lieu of the puppet show we have one youngish young man with a hideous name who hops into a taxi cab – for our purposes a kind of mini puppet theatre – to carry out a mission, a search mission, and with any luck at all this will clear up a lot of things.

(After the boy arrived in 'the West', moved to the western part of the country and settled in the western part of a city, he was sent to nursery school. The school was close to Blijdorp Zoo, so his class went there a couple of times a year. On the way they'd sing – feel free to join in – that old favourite:

Row, row, row your boat
Gently down the stream,
Merrily, merrily, merrily, merrily,
Life is but a dream.

And sing it over and over again until they reached the zoo. They'd get to look at all the funny animals with pointy ears or long necks or cuds to chew on. They were taken back to the zoo when they were older, but this time they'd been given a project:

— Look for a giraffe. What colour is it?
— Look for a water buffalo. Why does it chew its cud?
— Look for a penguin. Is the coat (a) shiny, (b) dull or (c) rough?

Now that he was out looking for his uncle, who might be anywhere, he felt a similar need for a questionnaire.)

A search mission? Look for what? where? who? A certain somebody who, on the day the Mercedes Benz 240D wheezed on to the highway with the boy in the passenger seat, had been declared missing. Or would be unless the boy found him. If the boy found him.

The uncle had elephant ears, like his brother. His hearing was sharper, but his wits were duller because: who would take off on the eve of a wedding, his *own* wedding, no less – the day a man's expected to stop hanging around the Parcheesi tables – and head for the very same Parcheesi tables where he had always lost to the Gimp?

Meanwhile, back at the house, the wedding guests were being plied with tea and beverages supposedly provided by the groom but paid for by his brother, and various meats smothered in various sauces supposedly provided by the man who, thanks to his marriage to a woman from 'the West' (a Dutch milkmaid with raven hair), will be allowed to immigrate to 'the West'. A wedding feast in a square house with a hole in the middle, in a village by the sea that hadn't yet tumbled off one of Iwojen's cliffs. The long wait had come to an end – that's how the boy saw it. So what kind of a person would cut off his ears to spite his face at a time like this? The future bridegroom, the uncle of the boy who'd hopped into the taxi, for a variety of reasons about a variety of things, that's who. So that the boy was obliged to go looking for him in the zoo known as Iwojen. Hopping into a cab hadn't been his idea, he hadn't wanted to go. Where was he supposed to look? He had been taught in 'the West' that when something goes wrong, you have no one to blame but yourself. But, he added, if you can't stand the heat, get out of the kitchen. Just as he had decided to make himself scarce, the father, standing on the lower-lying cactus field behind the house – the scene of the bread and raw onions – issued an order: 'Go find your uncle.'

Lamarat would never forget the tone in which these words had been spoken: humble, you might even say beseeching, over-excited, though not with joy – words so fraught with the fear of personal failure that they were about to knock the father out cold. (It looks like I'll have to play the father for a while, thought Lamarat.)

'It's still early. If he shows up before the evening's over, we'll be all right. Please go,' said the father with the elephant ears and Mafia face.

'No, I won't go,' replied Lamarat who had his mother's ears, thank god, but his father's brains, poor guy. 'Uh-uh, no way, I'm staying right here.'

Less than an hour later, perched on the leather seat of a taxi making its way down a winding asphalt road, Lamarat realized that he could only plea temporary insanity. Why on earth did I say yes? Did he yank me by the ear? Did he threaten hell and damnation if I didn't carry out his stupid orders? Nope. He could have yelled and screamed all he wanted, but I didn't *have* to go. So here I am, sitting in a taxi, in a car, and god only knows where I'm supposed to look for my uncle. How did that phoney macho manage to rope me into this anyway? 'Start with your cousin in Al Homey,' he said, 'and otherwise try Ammunir the Gimp. Ask the candy hawkers where he might be. Or else the cab drivers. Or the women who aren't wearing headscarves – they might know him. Just do *some*thing.' So Lamarat Minar went. His head was already filled with a rhythmic ticking that was slowly communicating itself to the driver: pup-pet-show, pup-pet-show. It didn't take long before Chalid's head began ticking too. Tickticktick a little puppet, and tickticktick another little puppet, it went. So what do you do at moments like these, when you're driving somewhere and you don't know where you're supposed to go and you feel like there's a sword hanging over your head that's just dying to fall? You start talking, like your lazy mother always does. Saying whatever comes into your head, blathering on about nothing. To whom? To a wall, a leather ball, a typewriter, or if none of these are available, a taxi driver. Spontaneously, on the spur of the moment, with no prompting. Which is how it came about that Lamarat found himself telling Chalid what had happened to him and his father and to a certain extent his mother but most of all to Mosa's future wife. Imagine the surprise of both the boy and the driver when they discovered, fairly early on in the ride, that the driver actually knew the uncle! 'One of my best friends – we used to go down to the beach together.' (And to the girls, but he only told him that after they'd recovered from their mutual surprise.) 'As a matter of fact I saw him just today . . .'

'When?' Lamarat shot out of his seat.

'Some time this morning.'

37

'What time, exactly?' He wouldn't have hesitated to rip the tongue out of Chalid's head if the time had been written on it.

'I don't know, kid, but in any case before the sun got stuck up there in the sky. Is this damned heat getting to you too?'

'Where, exactly, did you take him?'

'To F. You must know the place I mean – the border town where all the Africans hang out.'

'And where did he go after that? Tell me!'

'I don't know, kid. Mosa isn't much of a talker, you know. His talents lie in other directions . . .' (Short silence.) 'Anyway, it sure is funny, you being his nephew and all, and sitting right here in my cab,' he said, and he rolled his eyes. Oh great, a cross-eyed cabby.

Funny's the word, it was a riot, but the real comedy was yet to come.

But let's begin at the beginning, and recount the climb up Sugar Mountain.

The man who built a rocket out of matchsticks

It began in the morning, or rather, late in the morning, at approximately twelve noon to be exact. It began the moment the sun, looking as if it had been catapulted into the sky, reached its zenith and seemed to want to stay there forever. It began the moment Lamarat heard – or was it just his imagination? – voices whispering from behind the leaves, discussing the heat and the sun that never failed to shine; the moment the lizards crawled unseen from their holes and crannies to sun themselves on the rocks.

The bridegroom's disappearance from Iwojen on precisely that broiling hot day came out of nowhere, at a time when the temperature in the region had reached such heights that even the bamboo that usually nestled in the gullies had withered and died. 'It's unbelievable,' said Lamarat's grandfather to the wedding guests in his house, unaware that his son had vanished and that his grandson had been sent to bring him back. 'Gentlemen, it might interest you to know that the grapes aren't the only plants to have been hit – even the reeds are scorched. Anybody who goes outside today doesn't have the brains Allah gave a camel.'

One of the few people in that region who had noticed both the mysterious disappearance of the uncle and the heat plaguing the region that day was a fifty-eight-year-old taxi driver who was making his daily run over a winding asphalt road that snaked its way through the region known to the residents of the coast and nearby hills as Iwojen.

Think of Iwojen, if you can, as a place that has nothing to offer. No, I mean absolutely nothing. Perhaps you would find it more convincing if I told you about the sun, how it dried up everything in sight, sank into the sea at night, sucked up so much water and got so big that Lamarat was afraid it would explode in mid-air like an astronaut? Or maybe I should mention the steep bluff towering above Touarirt like a giant blackboard with grooves, and cutting if off from an indifferent outside world? Or shall I describe the clay soil in Touarirt's green valley, a series of cracks and crevices offering shelter to nothing but sun and air? Or shall I tell you about the village graveyard, Sidi Gallush, where, God willing, Lamarat's father hoped to be buried one day? Or the delta, that tiny green cunt on which the villagers had to grow everything they needed: potatoes, tomatoes, onions – delicious when served with lamb, a couple of which are bleating in every sheep pen? Or should I mention that no one has been living in the village since the wedding?

'They used to,' Grandpa would say, 'before they built the cinemas.' But now everyone has moved away and it's deader than a doornail. Not a soul in sight. Except on 13 July, when one house in Touarirt was crammed with pots and pans and people: the house where Lamarat had been born, where Mosa had been born. It was in that house, in an otherwise deserted village, that the groom had wanted to marry his bride.

Why get married there, uncle with the big nose and spindly legs, uncle of the jokes and pranks? Why were you, to put it bluntly, so all-fired hot to hold the wedding

in that deserted valley? 'Well, uh. . . well, uh . . . because
the other option was to have it in your father's house in Al
Homey, and to be honest my heart just isn't in that place.
There's nothing, and I mean not a doggone thing for me
there.' (On the other hand, as people like Chalid and
other interested parties knew all too well, there were
enough folks in Al Homey hoping to run into him for one
reason or another: 'Hey, Mosa, *amesian*, kid, where's the
money for the cigarettes you promised the sunflower-seed
vendors, the money for your bar bills, and most of all the
money for the girls – Turia, Malika, Mariam, Zuleikha,
Bahiya, Darifa and Chatischa, especially Chatischa to
whom you promised this, that and the moon, to whom
you promised a gold bracelet and a pair of earrings?
We've got your number, you deadbeat. You went around
raising hopes and shooting bull by the barrel. You can bet
your sweet ass that we, the bar-owners, the sunflower-
seed vendors and the girls you brought all the way from
Melilliar to Al Homey just to show off, haven't forgotten.
Is that why you skipped out, uncle? Be honest. Because
you were scared of the girl with the long eyelashes? Or the
one with the chipped nail polish and gold purse? The girls
you didn't invite to your wedding, even though they've
given you so much? The girls you told more of your
secrets to than you'll ever tell your wife? Were you afraid
they'd kick up a fuss at your wedding when they realized
you were pledged to just one girl from now on? Which
reminds me, you have been to see a doctor, haven't you?
About . . . you know, having something on your wuzza-
roo that might be catching? Of course you can't saddle
your so-called first and last with a disease you might
have picked up from that virtual-reality harem in Al
Homey . . .')

Quite a collection of curses and complaints. Well, what
can we say? If all those unspoken accusations, which

contain more than an ounce of truth, were to be aired in public, the uncle's jaw would drop. Things would be awkward, painfully awkward. His head would start spinning and ticking and giving him sleepless nights. But thank god the people who know these things also know the local mores. Isn't it fantastic that there's such a thing as convention? Unwritten rules, whispers, tittle-tattles coming from god-knows where and built into all the holes and cracks in the countless houses, lurking around the hushed and silent corners and pillars. One day someone will stand up – the Soothsayer, the Almighty, the Unbeliever? – and immediately sit down again – the Blind, the Deceitful, the Demagogue – and cry out with great strength of mind, 'Stop! If the shoe fits, take it off, because I'm the one looking for the tittle-tattles, the whole grab bag of innuendoes hidden in the house. You want to bet I'll find them?' And he'll go looking – in the pitch-dark because of course the lights won't be working – first with a matchstick, but that's no help, so then with a lighter, that's more like it, and after that a flashlight, keep going, you're nearly there, and finally with a lamppost clutched between his knees. You're getting closer, kiddo, search every nook and cranny and keep an eye out for cockroaches. And he'll find absolutely nothing. 'Whew,' he'll pant, the man from Alcatraz, the man hiding in the dark, 'glad I got away. At least I, Mosa, am safe. At least my house is in tiptop shape.' And to show that he knows exactly when the lights ought to be on and off, he holds the wedding in Iwojen. Milk and meat, city and country, wife and whore – if you want to be kosher you gotta keep 'em separate. That way it'll be safe, cosy, private, closed to outsiders. And you even get presents.

Maybe that's the reason Chalid ('He Who Knows All') wasn't invited. That hermit of the highway, fun at first and now a bother – ready ear to the thousands of souls who come and go from Touarirt and will one day return to silently demand their place in the family grave at the bottom of the village, that circle at the foot of Sugar Mountain, that Sugar Mountain a thousand times one thousand sugar mountains.

It was called Sugar Mountain because from a distance the flat bluff at the top resembled a sugar loaf. The association wasn't entirely coincidental. In the square house located approximately five hundred yards from the sugar-loaf mountain, on the day that the bamboo withered and died (as well as the day before that), several women and a man or two were busy wrapping dozens of sugar loaves in a tea towel (made in Taiwan) and tapping them with a small hammer (made in Germany) – the kind of hammer you'd use to bang a nail in the wall if you wanted to hang a clock. The wrapping and tapping of the spanking-white sugar loaves was part of a three-day marital marathon being held in the house located precisely five hundred and thirty-three yards from a steep dirt road.

What had Mosa said to the father? 'Just say the word, big brother. It'll save you money and I can bid a fine farewell to something I hold dear: Touarirt, village by the sea, do you know what I mean or don't you? What would a country bumpkin like me do in Al Homey, a place filled with parvenus like you, jumped-up ploughboys, yes you heard me: a bunch of nouveaux riches, and dumb ones at that! I've done my best for you and that house of yours, brother, and I only ask one thing in return: that my girl and I be allowed to spend our wedding night in the house by the sea.'

Mosa also managed to slip in a request for help later on in Ollanda – 'Enough so that I can take care of myself and that sweet gal, preferably somewhere in the same neighbourhood. No, brother, I'll get it together. I'm gonna make something of myself, you'll see.' (As it turned out, when the uncle finally did make his way to the north, via an alternative route, he began by doing odd jobs, and before long he was able to buy himself a car so that he could travel back and forth to France until he'd stashed away enough money for a snack bar, after which he was able to buy an apartment in Melilliar and so ultimately wound up back where he came from. One afternoon they found him walking past a line of cars parked along the road, drooling and spelling out the words NEW YORK to himself three hundred times. The last I heard, but then that was a couple of years ago, he'd been committed. Former friends, likewise candidates for the funny farm, went to see him, and I'll be damned if they didn't come back muttering, 'All he does is spell out the letters N-E-W-Y-O-R-K, it's unbelievable, it never stops the doctors say, he's at it night and day.'

Finally, after much pleading and deliberation, the brother waved away his wife's objections – she thought the whole idea was a disgrace – and agreed to the proposal. 'Listen, brother, what you're doing is pretty *hek-o-hek*. Nobody is dying to have a wedding by the sea, I can tell you that. The whole idea is pretty so-so.' Truer words were never spoken. All the father had to say was '*hek-o-hek*' and everyone in Iwojen immediately knew what he meant. One of the most salient features of the region is that it's *hek-o-hek*. Chalid often used that word in the cafés when he was pissed off, when he too had lost to the Gimp – whose game kept improving and whose hand was starting to take on the shape of a dice (the little rectangles on the ends of his fingers were beginning to wear off) – so that the taxi driver would flare up, especially after the second drag on his third gigglestick, when everyone was asking him when the hell he was going to buy another car, 'because, let's be honest, that Mercedes of yours, that bucket of bolts, is ready for the scrap heap.'

'I'll be the judge of that, I'll decide when and what I buy, and anyway that junk heap of mine is a sight better than you deserve, no kidding, you guys don't deserve a better taxi, because you know what you are: you're so-so. You can't even win from a cripple. Stupid, too stupid to notice the difference between anything at all . . .'

And the rest of the evening Chalid would mumble darkly, '*Hek-o-hek*, neck-and-neck, no-no, oh-oh, so-so.' To Chalid, *hek-o-hek* meant something like: all or nothing.

During the summer the daytime temperature in Iwojen rarely went below eighty-five degrees. And in the winter it was as if the clouds and torrential rains had taken up permanent residence and were in no hurry to leave.

'Do you know what I mean, Gimpy – all or nothing, that's what it's like around here, they either want to have everything or absolutely nothing.' And he said it more and more often, mostly to friends who were leaving – one of them off to seek a better life in the fishing industry, another heading north and a third simply moving away. The king of the winding asphalt road wasn't the only taxi driver in Iwojen, but he was the only one who had been born there. He knew his passengers by their first names, their last names, their nicknames. And it was Chalid, careful not to offend his paying customers, who thought the residents of Iwojen were so-so. 'The people around here are strange,' said Chalid. 'Off their rockers. If you say, Potatoes, they say, Beans. And if you say, Beans, they say, Onions. It's unbelievable.' But since he depended on them for his livelihood, he kept his mouth shut. For five dirhams per person Chalid would drive the people of Iwojen to the border town of F. To there and no further, since his licence didn't permit him to go beyond that point; so people would get out, and he'd turn the cab around, switch off the engine and wait until it was once again full of passengers needing to go to Iwojen.

For a long time F. had been a little village. Then, in less than two years, it had swelled into a small city, complete with school buildings and cafés. F. served as the gateway to the crown colony of Melilliar, a small enclave of Spaniards who neither can nor want to speak Moroccan, and Moroccans who only want to speak Spanish. Al Homey, the favourite of returning emigrants, was several miles down the road. It consisted primarily of houses, houses, and more houses, interspersed with an occasional photo shop, furniture maker's, mini-market and chicken slaughterhouse. The majority of the people from around Al Homey who had gone to 'the West' had used their francs, pesetas, Swedish krona or hard Dutch guilders – low interest rates had a favourable effect on the exchange rate – to build a house in Al Homey. Which is why so many people, particularly the merchants, complained about the non-foreign foreigners. 'They're arrogant, grasping, pushy, you name it. I don't like 'em, I don't like 'em at all,' said Lamarat Minar's cousin, a nice guy, especially since he was able to tell him where the uncle was: 'There's only one place he can do what he needs to do, and that's in Melilliar.' And without missing a beat he continued, 'During the summer you can't turn around here without bumping into one of those "foreigners", and in the winter it's so quiet the kids play out on the streets. But then we don't make the rules, do we, Cousin Lamarat, it's pretty so-so here, you know.' And yet the people in Al Homey loved the 'foreigners' – after all, they brought in hard cash, held wedding banquets, enabled the young men to go off and seek their fortunes, and the young women to stay at home for the rest of their lives, ordered houses to be built and tore them down again.

46

They put up mosques, put down carpets, hung black-boards, bore children, married them off and remained one hundred percent illiterate until the day they died. And how everybody adored them! Love is so beautiful when it's for sale, just ask Mosa the next time he's had a few too many. And if the cousin was honest – which he was when push came to shove – he'd admit that Al Homey had sprung up out of the womb of the 'foreigners' and that it suckled at their breasts.

The taxi driver likewise depended on the 'foreigners' for his livelihood. There were enough visitors who didn't have a driving licence and therefore had to rely on his Mercedes and navigational skills. But on the afternoon in which the taxi driver's eye was caught by a raised hand at the side of the road, just when the sun had risen to its historic heights and everyone in Iwojen, and I mean everyone, had taken refuge indoors in their cool houses, those square doughnuts dotting the landscape in groups of five, there were only two people still out and about: the taxi driver in his Mercedes 240D (made in 1978, imported from Belgium) heading towards the nearest city, the border town of F., and a young man named Lamarat. Chalid guessed that the young man, walking past a row of agaves somewhere in the vicinity of the old Spanish spring, was about twenty years old, twenty-one at the most. But it just goes to show you, as the taxi driver always said, that age doesn't mean a thing these days. Because why would a twenty-year-old kid be walking down an asphalt road in the direction of the border town of F. at the hottest time of the day, the week, the month, the year, or as the old folks would later say, in the last twenty years? Surely only someone with the mind of a child would do something so ridiculous, something so unlike an Iwojenian?

The boy, trudging along the winding asphalt road at

high noon, looking like he had come out of nowhere and was going nowhere, became aware of a droning crescendo behind him. He turned around and saw a car speeding towards him. Surprised, he stopped dead in his tracks – the last thing he expected to see was another human being. It was simply too hot for anyone to be outside at that hour. On his way up the hill from the village, which lay on the coast, he hadn't seen a soul. Not one single chicken, person or lizard had set foot outside farmyard, house or crack in the wall. The fact that someone had actually ventured outside, and in a car, surprised him less when he noticed the red sign on the bumper, which meant that the car bearing down on him was a taxi. He raised his hand and took two steps, all that was needed to get him to the shoulder of the narrow, hell-hot road. The driver, seeing the raised hand, slowed down, adjusted his mirror, stopped, and opened the door. As the boy took a seat, the driver realized why the kid had been walking down the asphalt road. His face, his clothes, the way he said hello, the way he moved – everything pointed to the fact that he was from the north.

Ever since he'd come up the hill and seen the figure standing there, the cabby had asked himself why someone would be out at that hour, and on an asphalt road, of all things. At first he thought it might be a mirage. When it was this hot, the road often gave off reflections; this wouldn't be the first time strange images had arisen in the quivering heat haze. It couldn't be a person, he thought. It was twelve noon, and the thermometer inside his car pointed to a hundred and fifty degrees, which meant that it was at least a hundred degrees outside in the shade. And in weather like this (ninety percent humidity: the driver felt it in every pore in his body, which was sticky with sweat), nobody went outside; even crazy people, and Iwojen had its share of them, stayed inside. So who oh who had been stupid enough to plunge into this heat? Whoever it was, his daring bordered on insanity, since he was walking down an asphalt road, and asphalt roads, as everyone around here knows, generate the most heat.

Maybe it's a ghost, thought Chalid, only to pooh-pooh the idea a moment later. Nonsense, I haven't gone around the bend yet, or at least I don't think I have, he philosophized as the dot danced up and down in the heat waves. Briefly Chalid considered accelerating so he could flatten the ghost on the highway. But luckily it was just a momentary flash, because the closer he got, the more the ghost took on a shape. The shape eventually materialized into a human being, and the human being finally appeared to be a young man who was obviously not from around here. Which may go far towards explaining why he was out walking on the hottest surface in all of Iwojen: he didn't even know enough to come in out of the heat . . .

Balala in the ropes

The driver often heard stories, stories about men who were driven mad by hashish, women who were visited by strange men on the twenty-seventh of the month, women who flocked to the city, mostly from the south, to capitalize on their legs, asses and snatches, which he was urged to go see for himself in Melilliar; but the story he heard from Lamarat had nothing to do with any of these things. Lamarat was clean in word and deed, of course, squeaky clean. That was something the driver knew for a fact because Lamarat lived far, far away in another part of the world, in a country where the temperature never soared to the heights it did here, where feverish words never reached his ears, where you never had to contend with the horniness of a hot summer. In other words, a country that never had to take matters into its own hands. It was in this privileged place that Lamarat lived in an apartment block in North Sesame Seed City. When he was still young and innocent, he used to amuse himself by filching things from school – what do you mean squeaky clean? Sometimes a pencil set, sometimes a book, and one day a box of chalk. Nobody at school seemed to mind, since nobody noticed anything was missing. Why not? the boy reasoned; there were more than enough pencils, storybooks and chalks. Their classroom alone must have had a hundred thousand exercise books and at least that many pencils. Every once in a while he dreamed he'd found the key to a school kleptomaniac's Valhalla.

The boy had swiped the chalk for sport. He had a stopwatch too, though he hadn't stolen it. He didn't steal from shops. The toy sector had been hit hard recently, subject to repeated takeover attempts by junior raiders who made a sport out of grabbing as many marbles as they could from display bins, stuffing them in their mouths and then running like hell. Most of the time it went fine; some of his classmates had so many marbles they could have opened up their own shop in smurfs, pirates, purple aggies and pink panthers. Now and then something went wrong. One of the pint-sized raiders would run too fast, forget to dodge around a display board, fall flat on his face, and swallow a dozen marbles. Most of the marbles would wind up in the oesophagus, though occasionally one would get lodged in a lung. Such things did happen, which is why the boy never attempted a daredevil stunt like that. Nobody at school noticed his raids on the supply cupboard, and you didn't have to put pencils, Grimm's fairytales and bits of chalk in your mouth. It made more sense to put them under your armpit, under your jacket or in your pocket.

Outside his apartment block, where Lamarat, his parents and his sister lived on the first floor, there was a pavement. The pavement ran from one corner to the other and was about fifty yards long, give or take a yard or two. Using his stolen chalk, the boy drew a line from the apartment door to the curb. Then he walked to the end of the street and drew another line of the exact same length. After that he started counting. There were a hundred and twenty-eight squares between the two lines. By adding approximately fourteen inches for the cracks between the squares, which were filled with weeds, the boy came up with a satisfying total of a hundred and twenty-nine squares. His next step was to call his sister. 'Hey, Rebekka, watch this!' She stuck her head out, yelled, 'Okay, monster, show me what you can do!' and watched as he walked to the corner, to the starting line by the front door, where he placed one foot on the line and the other just behind it and, leaning forward slightly, set his stopwatch. Then he flew to the other side of the world. On the first step he ran like a duck, on the second a donkey, the third a horse, and once he hit his stride he was running like the devil's own hellhounds, higher and higher, pounding the pavement, his arms pumping, back and forth, up and down, squeezing his eyes shut, saving the energy he needed to blink for his pounding legs, floating, screaming, raging, flying, thumping, spinning like a top and all the while thinking of the songs he'd learned from his schoolmaster, schoolmistress, schoolmisstrix:

> Twinkle, twinkle, little star,
> How I wonder who you are.
> Up above with a tin washtub,
> Scrubbing dirt a-rub-a-dub-dub.
> Twinkle, twinkle, little star,
> With a rocket you'll go far.

Squeezing out the last ounce, trying to feel the white spot in front of your eyes, so you know why you're doing it, trying to be the athlete he so desperately wanted to be: the gold-medal winner. And he'd cross the line, nearly crushing the stopwatch in his hand, look at the time, a tenth of a second faster, and think: I've gotta do better, I've gotta go for the best, for zero point zero zero. And he would walk back from the finish line to the start and turn himself around, so he could have another crack at reaching that high. And he'd repeat the whole thing. Over and over again. Until the sun went down, the moon shed too little light on the white line, and day was done, since you could no longer distinguish between a white thread and a black one.

The taxi driver who found the boy walking near the dried-up spring, the one that the Spanish rulers had built long, long ago – or at any rate before the driver had been born – never drove his cab into the village clamped between the thighs of the sugar-loaf mountain and the wet vulva of the sea. There was no way he *could* have got his car down there. The road was so narrow, bumpy, full of potholes and steep (a ten percent gradient) that hoping to arrive with all four wheels intact was about as realistic as your chance of picking up a girl from Deutschland. You could give it your best shot, knowing full well what the consequences might be, but in the end you'd never make it.

There were no serious consequences involved in stopping for the boy. Or so the driver thought. He was used to thinking in practical terms, especially when he was thinking about himself. This time his thoughts went like this: I'll stop for this kid, take him to F., he'll pay me the sum of ten doro (which is what the people of that region call half a dirham), and I'll drive back for the next fare. Just as he had brought another Iwojenian to the border town of F. that morning, just as he had been bringing people to and from the border town of F. for a hundred years. All you had to do was make the connection, shift gears and drive. Plus fill the tank from time to time and, most of all, not make things too hard on yourself. Anyhow, those were the thoughts of the taxi driver, up until the afternoon the heat caused the bamboo in Iwojen to wither and die.

So the driver picked up the kid, shifted into first, then into second, and shoved a tape into the tape deck. 'Those

54

crazy taxi drivers play only one kind of music in their cars,' a girl said to Lamarat years later. 'Every song is always about women, booze or mothers. It's all those machos ever want to listen to.' In the meantime he had discovered that the bit about the mothers wasn't entirely true. The only time he'd ever heard a song about a mother was that day when he'd been listening to the taxi driver's tape. Halfway through the number, the singer started calling on Allah at the top of his voice. At that precise moment, Chalid asked Lamarat how he was doing. He asked everybody who got in his cab how he was doing. You ask a woman how she's doing, you ask a man how he's doing, you ask old people how they're doing; you address everyone in a proper tone of voice and ask them how they're doing. But there's one thing you never do, and that's say what you think. Never, ever say what you think.

About the nuns and the bees

Few people in the country Lamarat came from were as quiet as he was. It always surprised him, and after he'd taken a shower, he'd wipe the steam off the mirror and, catching sight of himself, think: Well I'll be damned, it's true, mirror, mirror on the wall, who oh who is the most silent of them all? Me, huh? And then, proud of his inability to communicate with anyone whatsoever, he'd write his name with his big, fat middle finger on the newly steamed-up mirror: *L. the Silent.*

'Splash-splash' went the hands of Rebekka the Chatterbox in her mother's tummy (Lamarat may have mastered the art of silence, but Rebekka started talking in the womb and was a virtuoso blabbermouth). The splash-splash was strange enough, but what was even stranger was that one-year-old Lamarat, who was using his *yeme's* stomach as a pillow on the plane, was able to hear the splash-splash. 'Psst, psst, little screamer,' the tiny Rebekka (not quite seven months) said to her older brother, 'tell me where the heck we're going.' He had been crying and screaming his head off ever since they left Touarirt, even though from the moment the mother had walked out of the village and caught a cab that would take her to an airport in the desert, she had done everything she could to keep Lamarat quiet (on the path up Sugar Mountain she'd tickled him, while waiting for the taxi she'd made funny faces, in the taxi itself she'd let the child scream himself to sleep, in the transit lounge of Ouididiada Airport she'd puckered her lips and produced a variety of smacking sounds, in the ladies' room at the airport she'd nursed him, on the plane she'd devoted herself to the sport of tossing him in the air and catching him again, a manoeuvre that Lamarat tired of halfway so that he subsequently gave the milk back to his mother, and upon their arrival, gently cradled him), she'd done everything a mother can do to pacify a child, but even a mother is helpless in the face of such howls.

Still screaming and splashing – Lamarat screaming and Rebekka, in another attempt to make contact with her brother, splashing ('psst, psst, *buri* – I'm here, underneath you, dummy, dope, deaf as a post, why don't you listen for a change, splash-splash'), the two of them and their parents entered a house located somewhere in the middle of a city that Rebekka had been able to identify by its smell the moment they had landed: 'I smell, I smell . . . roasted sesame seeds, and yuk, I mean it stinks here.' And she moved her hands through the water again, making as many waves as she could to attract the attention of Lamarat, who began to suspect that something strange was going on; he abruptly stopped crying and screaming and turned his head from left to right, up and down, to discover the source of the sound that was making him pee.

Their father noticed nothing of pesky little Rebekka's splashing and attention-seeking. He brought them to their home, brought them home for good. 'Voilà, it's all ours, all yours, Jamina. Here's the living room, there's the bedroom, make yourself comfortable, the refrigerator's full and make sure there's dinner on the table tonight because I've got to go to work,' and he slammed the door behind him. Whew, he's gone, thought Rebekka, and she bonked against her mother's stomach again . . . 'Hey, Lamarat, you little twerp, are you out there, can you hear me?' And so Lamarat, who coūldn't even stand on his own two legs, found himself alone with a mother who liked to sleep late, a father who only came home when the potatoes were done, and a mysterious creature that kept sloshing around the placenta and umbilical cord and trying unsuccessfully to catch his attention. His glorious future as a Parcheesi player had been nipped in the bud. He had no choice now but to play solitary games. As soon as he was able to stand on his own two feet he started running through the house: through the kitchen, through the living room, through the bedroom. Endless rounds (mere prologues), games that went on night and day. Oddly enough, it was the father, who saw him the least, who was the first to notice that the boy had changed since he'd come to Holland, that he hadn't opened his mouth except to eat a spoonful of porridge or take a gulp of air when he could no longer breathe through his nose.

'Jamina, it's about the boy. I don't get it – crazy stuff going on when he was born, a crazy, crooked nose and now it looks like he isn't learning how to talk. Do you know what's happening, Jamina?'

Mother, the mother who was getting more and more attached to her washing machine and gas oven, wasn't the least bit worried. 'He's just clowning around,' she said (all the while thinking: Lucky devil, we came pretty close to having to feed his little corpse to the dogs). 'Like your mother says, he seems to have been born under a lucky star.'

'Is that your idea of explaining why he doesn't make a sound anymore? In Touarirt he used to scream loud enough to wake the living *and* the dead.'

'Humph,' said the mother, who thought her husband

was losing his marbles, 'only He-up-above knows what's happening, and sticking your nose in someone else's business is *haram*, so let's stop talking and go eat, before the potatoes turn to mush.'

And that was that. She got up to serve the potatoes, with artichokes and goat balls, while Rebekka (six months old) shouted, 'Hey there, folks, you should realize that he's upset, very upset, and all because of me. The little brat wants to know who's making all those funny splashing noises, splash-splash.'

Is that it? Had Lamarat been so impressed by Rebekka's water ballet that he'd permanently clamped his mouth shut so he wouldn't have to miss a single sound?

'Pooh, don't make me laugh. I've had twenty years of experience with these little chickadees and I can tell you this much: there's always one of those still-waters-run-deep types. When you play your guitar, hi-ho-the-derry-o, and clap your hands for them, those little eyes open up wide, but other than that you don't hear a peep out of them, not a peep.' Lamarat's teacher was nice and must have known which end of the stick was up since she added, 'But just wait till a girl comes around. Then our little Bob Marley – for some unknown reason his mother refused to cut his hair – goes wild, and so do the girls. It's like he's playing a game with them, though the cheeky little devil can't even count to ten.'

'Time you went to school,' his mother had said, shoving a brown banana in his hand and sending him off with the kid next door. There were twin girls in Lamarat's class, and he liked to show off, especially on the jungle jim. The twins called him 'Goofy' – another name that puts people on the wrong track – 'Goofy,' they'd say while he hung from his knees with his pomodoro ears showing and his arms across his chest. At the first sign that their interest in his gymnastic feats was flagging, he'd

60

switch to silly walks, animal sounds (elephants and dogs –
his speciality was donkeys) and, of course, tag. To please
them, he'd change into whatever they wanted; he'd have
turned himself into a tile if they'd asked. Often (every day,
every hour of the day) when Lamarat was horsing around
with the two sisters, he'd think: Do they know about the
splash-splash? Oh god, how can I explain it to them, how
can I explain that there's something, I don't know what,
sloshing around in my head? How can I make it clear to
them? But it was hard for Lamarat to make contact,
harder than dangling from his knees, so he gave up trying,
and the sloshing sound that sent him running to the
bathroom remained part of his inner world.

But you get older, your eyes open wider, and finally the
twins move away, leaving you behind with yourself and a
bunch of other cheeky devils who are just as quiet, have
just as much hair, count just as nicely to ten (one, two,
seven, nine . . .) and clump together as readily as filings to
a magnet. A magnet shattered by their fathers.

The breaking of the magnet was accompanied by the
breaking of the mother's water, a steady splash-splash
from which a little girl emerged. 'Here she comes, the
latest addition to the population of Sesame Seed City.'
From the moment the mother came home from the
hospital (room with a poolside view) and said to Lamarat,
'Here's your sis, give her a kiss,' the splash-splash in his
head disappeared and the heckling began. 'Ugh, you're
such a twit.' 'Watch out, buster, or I'll plaster your eyes to
the back of your head.' From day one of Rebekka's
residence in the Minar household, they didn't get along.
On the other hand, life was a bit easier because he was
able to pour his heart out to her. Oh, she might act like
she didn't want to hear all the razzmatazz and rigmarole
from the outside world, of which she caught only an
occasional glimpse, but when Lamarat stopped to catch

his breath and bring his adventures to a close, Rebekka begged him to keep on talking. About the little old ladies and the crab apples. 'Hold your horses, monsignor, you haven't told me everything. I want to hear more about those crazy dames.'

Hmm, what was the deal? Oh yeah, he hadn't wanted to go, but you know how it is, new friends, new experiences, united we stand, which loosens the tongues – and the hands, since one of the favourite activities of Lamarat and his buddies was spending late afternoons plucking crab apples along the Canal of the Wooden Apples.

'Oh, you know what it's like, it's spring, the crab-apple trees are full of fruit, so all you have to do is climb 'em, shake 'em and pick 'em, but Rebekka, what I wanted to talk about is this: have you ever heard of other religions?'

'Other religions – what're you up to now, Ratty, you'd better keep your hands off 'em, or somebody's liable to break your arm, but anyway, what's with these other religions?'

Lamarat stood up. 'Believe it or not, as you wish,' he said rather formally, 'but today I came in touch with another religion.'

'So? So small and yet so gutsy, you sound like that crazy uncle of ours, what's his name, oh yeah, Mosa, gosa, losa, another champion bullslinger, but tell me, what do you know about other religions?'

Lamarat could see in the eyes of his sister, as she peered over the edge of her bed, that she was curious, much too much in fact, and he wanted to keep that curiosity alive.

'Enough. A religion here, a religion there, and today I met up with the Christian religion, or to be more precise: the Catholic religion.'

'You dirty dog, you haven't gone all popey-dopey on

us, have you? Tell me, what's wrong with our very own honest upright Prophet? Well, tell me!'

Lamarat was one of those persons who could be made angry by overt accusations, sly digs and irrelevant asides. 'Whattaya mean? The churches around here are being turned into mosques, and you think I want to convert. No way! Besides,' he added in a small voice, 'the whole thing was a mistake on my part.'

Rebekka didn't have the faintest idea what he was talking about, so she asked, 'Where have you been, you sneaky Jesuit, you would-be *korayshely*?'

Where he had been was a couple of blocks away. On the Canal of the Wooden Apples and the crab apples, where he was dragged by his friends to the other side of the water. 'Come with us, magnet candidate, today we're going to bring you in contact with a different religion.'

To begin with, the other religion was old, positively ancient: three old ladies who ordered ten little boys to sit in a semi-circle. One by one the three ladies handed out three books, then lady number three handed out one more. The fourth one went to Lamarat, and he said to his sister, 'There was a frog in the middle of mine, in a pond.'

'Only one frog? Phooey, there are thousands of polliwogs in Touarirt's creek.'

'Yeah, I guess so, but how do you know that? Anyway, each of our books had a frog, and the women also opened theirs to a frog, so we had thirteen frogs in a row and a semi-circle, and the big frog in the middle dragged an easel with a big sheet of paper on it from the back of the room to the front and said, 'Okay, children, let's sing,' and we did, with the big frog on the left beating out the rhythm one-two-three-four and the big frog on the right moving her hands up and down, up and down, while the frog in the middle pointed from left to right at the words on the easel and we all croaked our hearts out . . .'

'And then the hymn was over. So tell me honestly, Ratty, how did you leave the room? Like you'd been born again?'

'Nah, I ducked out the back way. If you want to know the truth, the whole thing scared the bejesus out of me.'

Slippery Rat, thought Rebekka, and let him ramble on about the nuns, and about the chocolate milk and cupcakes, the bread and wine, which were passed out to the twelve remaining frogs.

Before long lots of other people were falling for religion, in fact they were falling in droves, and then one day, as was to be expected (Rebekka had predicted it: 'Mark my words, Lamarat, tomorrow he's gonna send you to one of those, uh prayer-bead schools or whatever they're called'), father came home with prayer beads in his left hand, an extra loud *sallam-u-alaykum* and the magic words, 'Ladies and gentlemen' (like he was in a café), 'it's darn well time for a darn bit of Islam in this house. From now on things are gonna be different around here.' And one of those things, aside from hanging up a *lomia*, a prayer calendar, and buying a big fat prayer book, was making Lamarat go to Koran school to learn about the Koran.

This meant classes held in the basement, the bowels, of a mosque that once upon a time, long before contraception, Thalidomide babies and the mass lay-offs that had sent the unbelievers scurrying back to Islam, had been a church. There were Koran classes on Wednesdays, Saturdays and Sundays. The father hoped the teachers would stress the importance of Islam to Lamarat and his classmates and teach him to reel off a couple of suras. Lamarat (laughed at by a snotty-nosed kid teaching herself how to race through the house and screaming, 'Lamarat's gonna get it, Lamarat's gonna get it, *ulla pulla*,' as he left the house on his first day carrying a slate and a piece of chalk) found himself in a totally unfamiliar environment.

Never before had he seen anyone – let alone a teacher – stuff mint leaves up his nose, but Rebekka refused to believe it: 'Mint leaves up somebody's nose, you gotta be kidding, man!' Never before had he seen a little boy with a wizened nose who liked to kill time – especially on Sundays, when the boredom had reached its peak – by meticulously picking his nose, kneading the bogeys into little balls and sticking them in his desk. Then he'd spend the rest of the day breathing heavily through his nose so he'd have more bogeys. At the end of the day he'd harvest his crop and knead them into a super ball, which he'd toss back in one go (Rebekka had no trouble believing that part: 'Easy-peasy, no big deal, I do it all the time'). Another kid had the delightful habit of sliding his hand, at the beginning of the lesson, under the waistband of his sweatpants, running his finger up and down the crack in his butt and then supposedly innocently waving it under the nose of his fellow classmates. Not that there weren't enough smells to contend with – thirty, forty or sometimes even sixty kids, girls and boys on separate sides, jammed into a classroom that couldn't have been more than fifteen feet long and twenty feet wide. Sometimes Lamarat had to go to the toilet, in which case he'd ask the teacher for permission to leave the room. It was the only Arabic word he knew: *mirhad*. Most of the time they let him go. The bathroom was upstairs, by the entrance to the prayer hall, which, Lamarat had been told, could accommodate up to two thousand people. However, only one person at a time could in all decency use the toilet. Actually, he only went in a dire emergency, when he knew he wouldn't be able to hold it in till he got home. That may sound silly, but presumably the facts will speak for themselves. You see, the toilet consisted of a hole in the floor, flanked by a white ceramic collar – a so-called Turkish toilet – surrounded by hundreds of white tiles to create the illusion of hygiene. The tiles were frequently covered from top to bottom with shit, which had been swept on, daubed on or smeared on in crude brush-strokes. Every once in a while there was even a message, as if a bungling graffiti artist had been practising his piece. Rolls of cheap toilet paper were stacked in the corner (Today's Supersaver: Ten Rolls For 2.99) and stuck to the tiles with the shit of the believers-to-be, who were down-stairs in the dank basement droning vowels while he was upstairs trying to leave the bathroom as quickly and as free from impurities as possible. Then he'd return to the classroom, where the teacher would be writing a sura on a rickety blackboard and expecting the pupils to write it down and learn it by heart. That's how the lessons went in the lower grades. There was also a teacher who taught them how to make their ablutions and pray. With a pointer tucked under his arm, he showed them how to bow to the north and told them how many times you had to bend over, how many times you had to kiss the ground, and at the end how you had to put your right hand on your knee, stick your forefinger in the air and rotate it round and round. (When Rebekka heard this she said, 'Is that the only thing they teach you nitwits? Sheesh, what kind of school is that?') He thought the prayer ritual was beautiful, and he felt a certain urge to imitate the teacher's example, but there was hardly time to practise, since the next item on the agenda was a test. They were tested at the end of every afternoon, or not at all, or only a couple of kids would be singled out – it depended on the teacher's mood. If they were going to be tested on a sura, one row of kids at a time would be asked to stand up and form a line behind the teacher. First the boys, then the girls, or maybe the youngest girls and then the boys. Or neither of these, depending on the will and whim of the teacher. Whoever had a turn was supposed to recite the lesson quickly and correctly, with no uhs and ahs. Any child failing to meet these criteria was ordered to hold out his hands. And wham. The pointer that had been firmly clutched under the teacher's armpit all day was put to work on the hands of the slow learners at a merciless tempo.

A funny thing about those pointers. They made their point all right, but they weren't necessarily made of wood. They might consist of two fluorescent lights taped together, or else have a rubber hose stuck to the end. The primary advantage of the rubber-hose variety was its reach. You could make it as long as you wanted, thereby solving the problem of those sitting in the back row or against the wall, who were beyond the reach of a hand or average-sized pointer. The hose clung craftily to your neck, while the red-hot poison flowed slowly down your spine to the rest of your body. In other words, it was a very useful and handy tool. A couple of teachers preferred thick planks of wood, which Lamarat thought were more humane – when your hand was smacked with one of those, the pain would radiate more evenly across the palm, and that was somehow more bearable. Still, not everyone shared his enthusiasm for the plank, because the number of blows was usually increased by way of compensation.

About the teachers (Rebekka liked teacher stories best): well, there was the teacher who walked around with mint leaves up his nose whenever he had a cold. And the teacher who never took off his leather jacket. And the teacher who only taught his own son, who had squeezed himself into a desk in the back of the room and would rock back and forth while trying to commit the entire Koran to memory. Which he finally did. So while the rest of the class was being disciplined by the teacher, the son got to go to Saudi Arabia.

'Wow, that school of yours is really a gas,' said Rebekka when Lamarat had finished describing the mosque. 'I can hardly wait to see it for myself.'

'There's no need for you to go. The man you marry will instruct you in enough religion to last a lifetime,' said the father with a phony smile. So Rebekka grew up knowing that one day she would have to wed some guy or other.

Rebekka's conversations with Lamarat became shorter, shallower and less coherent. After a while they were back to where they had started, and Lamarat heard only an occasional splash-splash.

Like the splash-splash of the sea. *The sea where she pledged her all, her heart and her liver too.* The sea where Rebekka whispered to the sleeping Mosa, 'One thing leads to another, you know' and 'It'll all work out, I still love you.' But perhaps I'm moving along too fast. First let's see if there are enough chairs for the guests.

Lawn chairs for sale

In the taxi, still on its way to Al Homey, Lamarat was mentally reviewing the list of people he had to see – Ammunir the Gimp and Cousin Camel Lamp, two people who might be able to tell him where Mosa was – when he suddenly said to Chalid, 'I've got problems here, problems back in the village, problems up ahead, and the thing about problems is, they're like food at a wedding banquet – you tend to bite off more than you can chew.'

Does that spoilt brat have any problems besides talking babies and Koran lessons? Chalid wondered.

'Pray tell me what those problems might be,' he said.

'What I'm worried about right now is the problem of the lawn chairs,' Lamarat said, and he laughed, then laughed again and said, 'My father brought a bunch of lawn chairs with him, thirty-three lawn chairs to be exact, so that the wedding guests would be able to eat better than they would sitting on the ground, but I'm afraid that at this very moment they're being swallowed up alive.'

'Oh Oracle of Touarirt,' an exasperated Chalid replied, 'Explain, I beseech you.'

'I think I've been as clear as can be, but okay: the lawn chairs that Pa brought with him are – just between you and me – of a decidedly inferior quality. Crummy plastic. I tried one out and, believe me, the legs start to go the first time you sit down.'

'What's it to you, lawn chairs, broken or unbroken? Other people see potatoes and you see beans, do you know what I'm saying or don't you?'

'The thing is that those lawn chairs have cost my father a fortune, and it hurts, it hurts extra hard, in your thighs, in your head, even your ears start ringing, when you realize that not only has your daughter's future husband skipped out on her, but a goodly portion of your fortune is on its last legs, do *you* know what I'm saying or don't you?'

Of course Chalid couldn't grasp the value of the lawn chairs, my dear Lamarat. Use your head for a change. How could Chalid possibly know that your father had combed the entire city for lawn chairs, sturdy, white, plastic lawn chairs that he could use to receive guests – 'Take a seat, *sidi*-whom-I-love-so-much, with whom I've been through so much, who will live, God willing, to a ripe old age, and by the way, what do you think of my lawn chairs . . .' – how could Chalid possibly understand that? To give him some idea, you'd have to show him where you live, the neighbourhood from which you set out for distant shores in the van with the thirty-three lawn chairs, the first of which broke en route when your father decided to test it ('Time for a little quality check') and took one of the four-legged critters out of the car, which was parked behind a Total station eight miles south of Dijon, and practically jumped on top of it with the full force of his considerable weight. Crack went the chair, snap went a leg, ripping the plastic, then the other three legs gave out. 'Please God let it be a manufacturing flaw, don't let it happen to the others.'

But it did happen to the others. (Yep, during the wedding. One by one the guests and the chairs buckled at the knees, so that by the end of the evening they were all seated on the ground, which was the local custom anyway. 'Ha!' the grandfather scoffed. 'That's what you get for trying to break with tradition. Fortunately you've had enough practice sitting around on your asses.') That was something he hadn't been able to anticipate when he'd watched their friends and neighbours loading their vans, stuffing their kingdom on wheels with lawn chairs, dozens of lawn chairs, thousands of lawn chairs, all heading south. 'When you get right down to it, we're doing a good deed; we're helping our parents, our brothers and sisters and all the others who have to sit on the ground and warm their backsides on the cold, pebbly earth, while we here in Deutschland stand helplessly by and watch our children's lives being destroyed by chairs: reclining chairs, swivel chairs, office chairs, TV chairs, even banana-bar chairs. Taking chairs back with you is a good thing, good for the people there – no more back-aches, no more hernias, blessed will be the poor in those little towns and villages, won't that be *fan-tas*tic?!' rattled the lawn-chair salesmen.

Where did all those lawn-chair salesmen come from? They sprang up just as suddenly and as rudely as their sales pitches. Fast-talking young salesmen, too slick for their own good, who'd figured out somewhere along the line that there was money to be made, lots of money tucked away in lots of living rooms, and started going door to door. ('Everywhere you see a roof rack, you got yourself a customer.') They learned a couple of words to help them get an even quicker foot in the door: 'Bow and say something in their lingo, it works wonders with these people.' One day, for example, Lamarat opened the door to a young man – 'Jacob-Jan, just call me Jake' – with a stack of lawn chairs behind him, who exclaimed, '*Sallam-u-alaykum, kane bak vie dhar!*'

'I suppose you think I speak Arabic,' Lamarat said, thinking out loud, 'but unfortunately I don't understand a word of what you're saying.'

'Oh, in that case, *ehlel ye sehlel ouid wewesch e mis n tefkecht*' (which freely translated from Berber means: Good afternoon, can I speak to your father, son of a king-sized portion of spite). You had to be brash with Berbers, even crude, Jake had been told, otherwise they didn't respond.

'Hello, what do you want?' asked the father, lured to the front door by the outrageous accent.

'What I want is none of your damn business, but luckily for me and for you too, I know what *you* want. Lawn chairs, my good man, I've got lawn chairs, and if you like I can also provide you with Van Nelle coffee and Sim Orange Juice, though I'm currently focusing on the lawn-chair segment of the market.'

'Thanks but no thanks,' said Lamarat, and he retired to the living room, leaving his father to look at one chair after another and listen to Jacob-Jan's jokes.

'Call me Jake, and I'll call you *abu*, you don't mind if I call you that, do you, *abu*? Anyway, what I've got here', and he whipped out one of the lawn chairs, 'is a chair that's absolutely unique, one of a kind. What makes it special? You're wondering what makes this chair different from the ones offered by my competitors? The difference, Ali, is that I understand you, that I know how dark and cramped the houses are over there in Moroccolala, what with those corrugated roofs and tiny little windows, you know, the kind of quarters that imply that space is a priority, ergo – you do know what 'ergo' means, don't you? – even one lawn chair is one too many. But never fear, they've ergonomically designed the heck out of these suckers, which means you can stack 'em up and get 'em out of the way much better than those of my competitors. And they're easy to keep clean – a little soap and water will do the trick – which is a real bonus in the desert where the sand is always blowing into the cracks and your women and daughters have to hose down the driveway every morning. You can't say I haven't done my homework, Ali. But of course you want to know if they're comfortable. No need to worry, Ali, even your wife, with that *shawerma* butt of hers, will find these genuine Dutch-made chassis roomy enough to accommodate her two airbags – or have they melted into one by now? Can you still get your piddler in there, Ali? Why, she'll feel like a princess without a pea under her mattress, if you know what I mean, Ali, or don't you read fairytales? Anyway, let's get down to brass tacks, since you're not the only potential customer on this planet. Are you going to buy one or aren't you, Ali, my friend?'

Father, dazed and impressed by the clever young man with the Donald Duck tie and wing-tip shoes who was such a perfect example of 'reverse assimilation', bought the lawn chairs. Dragging the damn things into the living room, he called to his wife, 'Honey, you won't believe what just happened. A man who'd fit right into Iwojen was at the door.'

Never before had the ghetto been worked by so many hucksters and had there been such a demand for lawn chairs as the year in which the bamboo withered and died in the gullies. Every year there was a product that was popular with the hordes of holidaymakers. Last year's hit had been the 'refrigerator'. The year before that it had been the 'cooker'. This year it was the 'lawn chair'.

Never before had so many lawn chairs migrated so far. Within weeks the homeland of the van owners would be teeming with white plastic lawn chairs from various discount stores, bargain basements and flea markets, where the price of an average lawn chair – three years old, no scratches – soared to dizzying heights in the weeks prior to the annual trek. There was such a feeding frenzy that a shortage threatened. The entire neighbourhood considered it a disgrace. Department stores and garden centres had to turn away flocks of customers who had decided not to go on holiday this year, but to stay home and buy a set of lawn chairs instead. The exodus of the lawn chairs, strapped to the roof racks with their legs in the air and covered with a tarp, reached such proportions that Consumer's Guide wondered where this was all going to lead and what would happen to people in desperate need of new lawn furniture. Those already in possession of lawn chairs merely shrugged; too bad they couldn't take even *more* with them. But since the matter had been featured on the eight o'clock news, the father of the son decided to play it safe: the night before they left, the boy would bunk down in the car. That way no envious neighbours would be able to remove the tarp and make off with the lawn chairs.

So on the eve of their departure, the father ordered Lamarat to take up his position in the car. He yelled to him casually from the kitchen, where he and his wife were discussing the upcoming wedding. Scepticism prevailed. For once the father and mother saw eye to eye. This was highly unusual. As Lamarat knew all too well, his parents rarely agreed about anything. Right now, the mother was dead set against going down there in the orange Mercedes van that the father had just purchased. She hated the colour orange. Besides that, he hadn't consulted her beforehand. The reason she hadn't been consulted beforehand was that the deal had to be settled fast. So fast that there was no time to ask a woman's opinion. While the father was talking loudly in the kitchen and watching his wife's hennaed hands make meatballs, kneading them into little golf balls and throwing in a pinch of Hamburger Helper, Lamarat tried to figure out why his parents were so averse to the wedding. The father thought the groom had no business getting married in an out-of-the-way village curled up in the thigh of Sugar Mountain. Nobody in his right mind would make the trip. Wagging his finger in the air, as if he were addressing his kid brother, the father explained in a gruff baritone that veered into an occasional tenor, why Touarirt was such a bad choice: in the first place it was too far away, a good fifteen miles from Al Homey, where the bulk of the in-laws lived, and in the second place it was totally unsuitable as a venue because it was impossible to get to. Mother dropped one ball after another in the oil – a hole in one, thought Lamarat – and, rolling up the sleeves of her dress, nodded in agreement and said, 'Anyone coming from Al Homey will have to take that asphalt road that winds through the hills and woods. Not even a donkey can negotiate that without twisting its ankle. So who's going to do that? Nobody but a simpleton, that's who.'

'Simpletons like us,' said the father. 'We'll be the only ones rattling around that house of his and trying to pretend nothing's wrong.'

'Exactly, you won't find me sending up a cheer for that young man,' said the mother. She stopped, switched the fan to three when she noticed that the kitchen had begun to reek of olive oil (El Ouzzania, made in Morocco, 9.99 a bottle, recommended retail price only), and said, 'You know what I think?'

'No, what, Mina?' said the father to tease her (he always called his wife Mina when she was about to speak her mind).

'What I think is that your brother is hoping in that stony heart of his that we'll fall flat on our faces, do you know what I'm saying or don't you? He knows that if he marries our daughter he'll be tied to us for the rest of his cruddy, miserable life, so he's getting back at us by making sure we'll break our necks on those rocks and boulders. It's not enough that he wants to bleed you dry financially, he also wants you to break every bone in your body, and please don't tell me how awful I am.'

The father had nothing to add. He took a fork out of the drawer, stuck it in the frying pan and took it out again. The fork had sunk its teeth into a brown meatball. Cramming it in his mouth, he said, 'Whah ii gfmink is nmawt imporwamnt.'

Not long afterwards, approximately six hours later, they took off, well-rested and well-fed, for the land of she'll-be-coming-round-the-mountain-when-she-comes, dum-di-dum.

If you want a family feud . . .

Lamarat couldn't stand the wedding he was attending, he told Chalid. Lamarat definitely couldn't stand the food being served at the wedding. He couldn't stand lamb's head and all those organs, which was beside the point, but he told Chalid anyway.

'Two bites of the cheek, and I'm full. And those bowls of guts are swimming in grease!'

Lamarat couldn't stand his mother. She stank to high heaven when she was wearing those strange perfumes. Lamarat couldn't stand his sister either. She stank even worse, and she hadn't been able to keep her mouth shut since the day she was born – or even before. She was a noxodorous cocktail of Chanel No. 5, Anaïs Anaïs and mashed Chiquita banana.

Lamarat – busy gazing at the sea dancing in and out behind the hills – didn't know what weddings were like in the old days, thought the cab driver. The way the girls would sneak off, and how he'd enter them, sliding his gearstick into their steaming, slit-open peaches, moving faster and faster until they'd say, in those sweltering voices, 'Take me from behind, you can save the other one for later.' At which Chalid would hiss, 'You bitch, God gave you that hole for shitting, not for my cock,' and he'd

77

quickly tuck it back in his pants. 'You I can do without,' he'd say, and push the girl away.

What else could he tell him: how the groom's mother would invite the bridal pair to drink a glass of water and sample the honey when they arrived at the house. There wasn't all that much to see. Except for a bunch of old maids banging on a drum all day until their fingers turned red.

The boy had no problem with his father. He was shouting along with a hundred other men and pretending he was better than he'd ever been in his entire life, forgetting the beer, the babes and the pork sausages he'd stuffed himself with over the years, forgetting everything except the absence of his brother, the bridegroom.

The boy didn't feel like eating lamb's balls. Unlike his sister, who would polish off about twenty of them by nightfall. With bread, no less.

The boy was told to shunt bowls of almonds back and forth between the men's section and the women's section. And pistachio nuts for his sister – she had eaten a pound of them, shell after shell after shell.

The boy was asked to take the young children behind the house to relieve themselves by the cactuses, his mother and father's former love nest.

The boy was sent out to see who was coming down Sugar Mountain. His mother came over every five minutes with a young child at her side. He was standing on a boulder that served as a lookout post, peering over the fig and pomegranate trees. 'I don't think anybody else will be coming, but keep your eyes peeled, and while you're at it, why don't you take this child down to the cactuses.' She had apparently forgotten it was a sacred place.

Lamarat saw that no one else was coming and dutifully told his mother. He didn't add that none of the children had peed.

Lamarat was the errand boy and conversational catch-all, which is why he was sent to ask his uncle to come to the men's section and shake a few hands. On the way his mother handed him a cup of tea. She was sailing back and forth across the courtyard: one moment she was heaping meat on a platter and the next she was heaping praise on herself for owning a house in Al Homey. As she gave her son the glass of tea, she praised herself for making such good tea. And then she praised herself for having a son. 'Born a month too soon, but you wouldn't know it to look at him now,' she flung in his direction, and the women who heard her burst into a loud chorus of blessings and wishes.

The boy went into the room the uncle was supposed to be in, the same one in which his lazy mother had given birth to him. He nearly had a heart attack. For some inexplicable reason the uncle was gone, gone from the room, and five minutes later he knew the uncle was also gone from the house. 'Do you understand how a thing like that can happen?' Lamarat asked Chalid. 'I looked everywhere, by the cactuses, behind the fig trees, but he was nowhere; he'd done a Houdini, incredible.'

'Maybe he was out taking a leak and you guys didn't see him because of all the cactuses.' The boy didn't answer. Anything's possible, thought Chalid as he carefully took a slow curve in second gear.

Mother, father, grandfather, grandmother, sister – dear sister – and the rest didn't know it yet. Anyway, Lamarat was standing there in the courtyard with the glass of tea still in his hand, looking at the women and the mother who continued to ooze and sweat. They didn't know what was happening, they had no way of knowing what was happening, they were too busy babbling about the bridegroom. No one had noticed a thing. Lamarat walked back inside and downed the glass of tea.

He went outside with every intention of telling his

mother that the uncle was gone. The mother took the glass from his hand. 'He must've been thirsty.' She slipped the glass into a plastic dishpan filled with soap-suds. 'Does he want another one?' His first response was hesitation, then doubt, and finally 'no'. He went to his father because he knew that his mother would explode if he told her the uncle was gone. She'd keel over in a heap, her skin would absorb all the perfume, and she'd be asphyxiated. (That was one way of getting rid of the smell, but thoughts like that weren't good for you.) To make it even more complicated, if he told his mother, every woman in the courtyard would know it within seconds. They'd recoil in horror, like a flock of goats that had seen a snake.

Inside, in the crowded men's section, glasses were going from hand to hand and hands from plate to plate. Tea leaves were stuck to every glass. A fly freed itself from the fly-glutted ceiling and began buzzing around a glass. The art of catching flies, thought the boy. One day, ten years ago, his uncle had taught him a trick. Two tricks, no less.

How to catch flies: when you've finished your tea, put your glass on a table. Flies are drawn to the glass. Flies fly into the glass. Grab the glass and quicker than you can say fly – or rather quicker than the fly can flee – turn the glass upside down. You'll have caught yourself the umpteenth fly of the day.

A lot of flies had been invited the day of the wedding. A whole lot of glasses and hands would be needed to catch them all. Perhaps the other trick, the hand clap, would work. One fly in the air, two hands in your lap. The fly lands on the table. Bring your hands to about ten inches above the fly and slowly lower them. The fly flies up and you clap your hands. Like you would at the theatre: with conviction. If you've done it right, the fly is dead.

Maybe, thought the boy, the best solution would be to ask my mother and the other women to raise their arms. The stench, the steamy wet spots reeking of Dior or some cheap imitation, ought to be enough to effect a short but sweet genocide of the little pests.

The boy left out the bit about the flies and the armpits when he was talking to the driver. What he did say was that he went outside, postponing the moment he'd have to tell his father, and sat down behind the wall, on the other side of the cactuses, to contemplate the groom's disappearance. Something had gone wrong, very wrong.

'It's funny, but I felt like I was my uncle, that I was carrying his burden. I think I'd feel the same if my father was sick or my mother had broken her arm. Even though I wouldn't want to, I'd feel like I was the one lying in bed or walking around with my arm in a sling.'

After that Lamarat stood up and went to the men's section with his heart pounding. He motioned for his father to follow him out back.

Bear with me for a moment while I play the role of the father who listens to his full-grown son speaking in rapid telegraphese: 'Uncle stop gone stop not in house stop absolutely certain stop looked everywhere stop what should we do stop.' And just so that it's perfectly clear to the father, he repeats: 'UNCLE GONE STOP STOP STOP DO YOU KNOW WHAT I'M STOP SAYING OR DON'T YOU STOP'. The father didn't know. However he did know a lot of songs from his bachelor days, one of which had the catchy title 'If You Want a Family Feud, Marry Me'.

> If you want a family feud,
> marry me, marry me.
> If you want a family feud,
> marry me, marry me.

The tune began slowly in the father's head but skidded to a stop when every circuit in his brain went haywire and his ears turned red. 'What's that you said? This is no time for jokes, I hope you're not joking 'cause if you are . . . 'cause if you are . . .'

'It's no joke, Father, he's gone, vanished, vamoosed, split, do you know what I'm saying or don't you?'

Of course the father knew what he was saying, knew so well that he felt like dancing, like singing:

> If you want a family feud,
> marry me, marry me.
> If you want the shit to hit the fan,
> marry her to a cream puff of a man,
> a cream puff of a man.

Father, whose shoes we've momentarily put ourselves into, quickly calculated the best way to do as many things as possible in as short a time as possible, so that no one other than himself, his son and God would find out more than they already knew.

What are you going to do (switching over to the boy's head since his thoughts are equally entertaining) – pretend you're Santa Claus, prance around the courtyard with a tambourine, stand on a stool and tell Iwojen jokes?

But to understand what happened next we have to go back thirty years, to when the father left the village of Touarirt in the Iwojen region. To when the father was being transported to the border town of F. where he could get a taxi that would take him to Al Homey so that he could catch the bus to Ouididiada Airport and board a plane that takes people to other countries and brings them back again in an endless cycle.

*

In the taxi the taxi driver – Bucket of Bolts Chalid, always in the mood to talk and younger then though his teeth were already in an advanced state of decay – said to the father-to-be: 'So you're going to Germany, hmm.'

'Deutschland is beautiful,' the father replied. 'It's green and there's plenty of work. You could be a paraplegic and they'd still find something for you to do.'

'So you're going to Germany, hmm,' said the taxi driver.

'That's right, Deutschland, they promised I could, and if anybody breaks his promise to me, I'll knock his block off.'

'So you're going to Deutschland,' said the taxi driver.

'It'll be my country, a good country, good money, hard work, success. I can't tell you how sick I am of all those Parcheesi games I've had to play over the years, how sick I am of slaving away for next to nothing. You know me, I want to prove myself and make sure my sons won't have to spend their time throwing dice in a café.'

'So you're going to Deutschland,' said the taxi driver.

'I'm going to Deutschland, we're going to Deutschland, and one day my children will be going to Deutschland, to see where their father used to work, the steel factories, the slaughterhouses, the high-rise apartments. They'll be proud of me. I'll send them there so they won't forget what I did for them.'

'So you're going to Deutschland,' said the taxi driver for the last time as they drove into the border town of F.

The young father got out and searched his pockets for five dirhams. 'Hang on a minute, Chalid, I've got it here somewhere.' He stuck his hands in his trouser pockets and felt around.

So you're going to Deutschland, thought the taxi driver, and you don't even know where your money is. You must be a total jackass.

'Give me a minute, taxi driver *sidi*, it's here somewhere, I put the cab fare in my pocket where I could find it, I know I did.'

The father finally found the money in a place he'd long forgotten by the time he and his son stood staring at each other, but the taxi driver's words had been engraved on his memory ever since: 'Next time, in Deutschland or wherever you wind up, always try to have some cash handy, so people won't think you're a poor slob from some backward country.'

The father had nodded, 'Hell of a good tip,' and slammed the door shut. The taxi driver turned the car around for the return trip and leaned out the window to pass on one more bit of advice to the young father.

'If I were you, I'd go to Ollanda,' he said, and stepped on the gas.

Thirty years later, the cabby's tip came bounding back like a deranged bouncing ball; never before had the father felt such a need for cash, for ready cash, preferably in his pocket. He stuck his right hand in his left pocket and pulled out a hundred-dirham note. 'Here' (handy as all get-out, thought Lamarat), and the father pressed the hundred dirhams into his hand, 'for the cab.'

'What do you mean, Father?'

'What I dammit don't give me any of your lip mean is that you're going to go and look for your uncle.'

'But where is he? Where could he be?'

'I don't care where he is, you're the one who's going to find out and it better be fast. Don't say another word, just go, go, go!'

So Lamarat went forth and searched and conquered nothing and no one, but he did bring back his uncle. Stewed to the eyeballs, and stewing in his own juice.

It was Grandma who opened the door

Now that Lamarat has found his uncle, it's time to account for the period between the arrival of the Minar family and the wedding itself. There were exactly seven days between arrival and wedding, five of which were spent in Al Homey, located fifteen miles from the village with the sugar mountain, which is roughly ten miles from the border town of F. and just under ten miles from the crown colony of Melilliar, where the Minar family had landed. In eight hours a boat from a harbour in the south of Spain had ferried them – the father, the mother, the boy and the sister – to another Spanish harbour in the north of the country they came from and whose mountain they still had to come round when they came, dum-di-dum.

They had left from Escorial, spent the night in cabins with showers and arrived the next morning fresh and clean. They were all, except for the orange Mercedes van, as clean as could be. The mother of the family had swiped a towel from the boat, the way her son used to swipe pencils from school, though the mother had slipped the towel into a plastic bag. Later on during the wedding the towel would be used to wrap up a sugar loaf. The boy hadn't seen his mother take it. What he had seen that morning was his grandfather waiting by the dock where the ferryboat, called the *Transmediterrania*, had landed.

Lamarat saw the grandfather in the middle of a throng

of people looking for their loved ones and waiting eagerly for stories and presents. The gifts came in a variety of shapes and sizes. Some families came from the north bearing butter. To ensure that the butter would survive the hot journey through France and along the coastline of Spain, they would fill two and a half gallon buckets with butter that they had purchased from a farmer (there were plenty of farmers in the polders around Gouda, Bleiswijk, Berkel and Delft willing to make a fast guilder by selling dairy products – not to mention sheep and an occasional cow – to bearded men in bright C&A slacks), and they would then take the buckets to the friendly butcher on the corner, who would store them in his freezer without charge though not without resentment, since they took up so much space, until it was time for them to leave on their holidays. But they were loaded down with other little gifts too: VCRs TVs, bicycles, and – very popular the summer the boy landed in the harbour – lawn chairs. For the most part these items were given as presents. Still, there were those who managed to do a pretty brisk business: men (and overactive women) who ransacked flea markets, surplus stores and car boot sales in search of items that would fetch a good price in the south. These would then be resold at flea markets throughout the city. Some people, undeterred by the stiff import duties, brought cars and left them behind. Other people brought money, and still others brought their sons or daughters, and sometimes even their sons *and* their daughters, and gave them away. Relatives from the city would come to collect the youngsters from the boat.

The father of the boy who had landed in the harbour that morning and was looking for *his* father, whom the boy had spotted right away, had also brought something with him: his willingness to organize and finance the wedding of his younger brother.

One by one the cars emerged from the ferry and joined a long line snaking its way through a cordon of people. Every couple of cars a person would leap out from the cordon. Recognition, Lamarat observed, was total and overwhelming. Sometimes the driver would stop the car and get out to give his father or his cousin or whoever it was a hug and a kiss. They would practically smother the poor guy in kisses, and some of them probably would have gone on all day, except that a surly Spanish customs official ordered them to put an end to the tender embraces and move on, since there were hordes of people without cars waiting for people with cars.

The van belonging to the boy's family finally rolled off the ramp. They had hardly driven a few yards on the continent of Africa before a small, grandfather-ish man broke through the wall of waitees and raced towards them. He gathered up his jellaba and hopped into the car. Laughter rose up from the little man's throat and he slipped in next to Lamarat with remarkable agility. One look and you were instantly reminded of a clown: two big ears, a tiny, wizened head and a grin from ear to ear. Grandpa, Grandpa, we're here at last! Everyone started talking at once, and Lamarat was bombarded by a cacophony of voices, a coming and going of words and welcomes. As they drove, the grandfather kept telling the father where and how to drive. They went through Melilliar, past a roundabout, until they could go no further and were forced to join a long line of cars. In the meantime Grandpa had distributed the required number of kisses. The boy had also had his share. Grandpa, smelling of lavender soap and olive oil, hadn't changed a wrinkle in the last ten years. It had been exactly ten years since the boy had been back to the land of his birth, and the grandfather had apparently taken a rain check on ageing. The only difference was that the furrows in his face were a little deeper, but when he smiled, which he did often, the lines were softened.

'May God watch over you, I'm glad you've come.'

'How's everybody doing?' Lamarat's father asked. The grandfather's reply leapfrogged over Lamarat.

'We're fine, Grandma's fine, sister's fine, I'm fine too.'

'And how's ole paleface?'

'I saw him yesterday. He said that the sea was calm and asked what time you were supposed to get here.'

'Is he staying in the house?'

'No, he went back again. Like he always does. He comes every other week, buys what he needs, visits his friends and then us, and before you know it, he's gone again. We're going to have to bring a lot of things to the village, son. A diesel engine to generate light, plates, bowls, beverages, and of course the most important of all: we'll have to buy some sheep and slaughter them . . .'

Grandpa went on reciting the list and would undoubtedly have spent another five minutes summing up various and sundry chores if the father hadn't cut him off, just a shade disrespectfully.

'How much are the damn sheep gonna cost?'

'You're out of luck, the price has gone up.'

'I knew it,' Lamarat heard the father say, 'I knew it.' Whenever the father was annoyed or had to think hard about something – for example how much he was going to have to pay for ten sheep – he'd narrow his eyes and press his lips together until he was one giant grimace. He had a coarse face, and at moments like these he looked like a big, overgrown Bert from Sesame Street.

The boy tried to pretend that the conversation was about a subject that interested him too. Sitting between the grandfather and the father, he followed the words from voice to voice the way tennis fans follow the ball from side to side. In the meantime he scratched his hair

88

and wiped away the beads of sweat on his forehead that had come up out of nowhere. Damn, it was hot, and he seemed to be the only one who knew it. Maybe it was because he'd been dying of thirst ever since they landed. With a thirsty look in his eyes, the boy turned to his father.

His father was balding, had been for years. It was possible that his hair might keep falling out until there was none left and he'd decide to let the hair on his chin grow. After a year of trimming and rounding off Operation Beard, he would be ready to buy a set of beads, say his prayers, memorize a couple of suras and go on a pilgrimage. Perhaps the father's life consisted of adapting himself to the amount of hair on his body.

The boy scratched his head again. He could tell from the way his father was sitting that he was annoyed. The father had assumed responsibility for the wedding arrangements and was footing the bill all right. But he had no choice – without him there would be no wedding.

The customs queue was getting shorter. Inside the van, the grandfather was busy passing on family news in handy gossip format, while outside a procession had formed: female beggars with babies strapped to their backs and young men who were going from car to car and nervously toying with stacks of forms and gnawed biros. The majority of the women were young, and the babies on their backs were swaddled in what appeared to be old sheets. In groups of three or four, they went from one car to the next, holding out their hands while looking beseechingly into the eyes of their sisters. 'You there, Fatima, from the golden north, no, don't pretend you don't see me, because I know you do, you aren't going to send me on to the next car empty-handed, are you, not when the women in the other cars have been so generous?' This heartrending appeal to their charity was too much for most of the women – they thrust a handful of change through the window or gave the supplicants a towel that had been used during the trip. All contributions were accepted. The money was tucked under a green or white caftan, and the towels, often with a greasy tuna smear still visible, were stuffed into a bag. Working their way down the rows of cars, the women finally got near the Minars. 'Don't give them anything,' Grandpa said. Why not? the boy wondered. 'Those aren't real babies,' Grandpa went on, 'they're dolls, and when they're through they take off their rags and put on decent caftans.' Grandpa's words evidently made little impression on the mother because as soon as the women reached the car, the Good Samaritan in her stuck out its hand and tossed a towel through the window. It was a blue towel with a white border (made in China) that had been purchased back in Ollanda. Shaking his head nonono, Lamarat looked at his mother. She was apparently embarrassed by her unusual generosity, because she gave him a girlish laugh.

The colourful column of beggars continued down the line, followed closely by the pack of young men in jeans and rayon shirts with dozens of forms in their hands. 'Give me your passports,' said the grandfather. Without a word the father gave him the passports, which the grandfather passed on to the young man standing beside the car and staring fixedly at the customs office. 'They'll fill in *la fiche* for you, the document that shows you've entered the country. We're going to let him take care of it, 'cause we'll get through customs a lot quicker that way.' Personal care was apparently not very high up on the young man's list of priorities – he hadn't shaved, and the whites of his eyes were so red that they looked infected. Of course you could do it all yourself, thought Lamarat, anybody could, but for a small cut these guys will whisk you through customs. Lamarat saw him write something in a few short, quick strokes of what he assumed was Arabic. Then he gave them back the form and said he'd see them at the customs office. Two hours later, the queue had shrunk, but Lamarat's thirst had grown beyond belief.

At around noon they were almost there. People were walking back and forth along the line of cars. Off to the side Lamarat saw a group of jean-clad men sitting on beer crates or upturned buckets. At first he thought it was an ad, but as the car got closer, he saw that it was for real. The men were holding bottles or cans of foamy bliss. Rivers of beer, Amstel oceans, were flowing through their fingers. Every other second, one of them would stand up, put his can down, start to say something, forget what it was, and sit down again. Then the next guy would take a turn. The people in the cars looked out their windows at their fellow countrymen, cavorting with Bacchus at the gateway to their fatherland. It almost seemed like they were deliberately thumbing their noses. After all, a few yards away, on the other side of the border, they could get their jaws broken for the same offence. So what did Lamarat feel like doing? He felt like leaping out of the car and joining their little game of sit down, stand up, sit down again. And all because of his enormous thirst. No water? Then a beer would do. No beer? Then a game would do. Anything to help pass the time and make you forget the wait. Just then the budding beard-wearer released the hand brake and they roared up to the checkpoint. The guy with the passports popped up beside the van like a jack-in-the-box. He ordered – unbelievable! – the father to accompany him to the customs office. 'I'll do the talking, you hold the passports, and oh yeah, don't forget to bring your wallet.'

Palms greased and passports stamped, the father put

away his wallet, released the hand brake and drove into their homeland.

Whoopee, we're here. And what's here like? Dust, donkeys on one side of the road and trucks on the other, all trying to worm their way into Melilliar. Rush hour in Iwojen, with everybody going honkhonkhonk and why don't you get a move on, you asshole, you son of a whore, father of a whore, haven't you figured out how to drive yet!

Little boys, the kind who spend their evenings in Parcheesi joints, are walking up and down the rows of cars with cartons of cigarettes, singing in chorus: 'Casawinstonbest-casawinstonbest-casawinstonbest, three kinds of cigarettes oh you want a pack of Marlboro if you wait a minute sir I'll get one from the café across the street no I don't earn a thing on the sale but while we're at it how about a bottle of Sim Orange Juice or maybe I can get you something else.' But what about the people who don't smoke and aren't thirsty? They do without and talk about this, that and the weather, about meat and butter, cats and dogs. About nothing, in other words. Like Grandpa and the father. Wedding this, wedding that, have it here, have it there, no, he won't. The car turned yet another corner. Jumping jehosephat, it's *hot*!

On to the highway. How far do we have to go go go? Lamarat kept seeing young kids on the side of the road, sitting on rocks by stacks of black buckets filled with red, yellow and green prickly pears. For a couple of dirhams you can have an entire bucketful. Make sure you check the bottom of the bucket to see if they've stuck the rotten ones underneath. Lamarat adored prickly pears – or so his mother said. 'But watch out for the prickles on the inside, son, as well as the ones on the outside. Here, give them to me, I'll peel them for you.' Prickly pears were apparently bunger-uppers. They could play real havoc with your bowels. Back then, ten years ago, when his grandmother would see him sitting in the courtyard and stuffing ten or fifteen of them into his mouth, she would raise her fist and wave it around as a warning. 'It's not the same as eating a bowl of peanuts, my grandson, be careful, before you know it your insides will be a mess.'

Everyone wanted to know how Grandma was doing. 'Fine,' said Grandpa, 'Fatma's doing fine.' And so they wheeled into town, talking about grandmas and grandpas, horses and donkeys, stones and sunbeams. The car curled itself around one corner after another until the father finally said, 'This is it. We're here.' What Lamarat saw for the first and presumably last time was this . . .

. . . Tucked away in the shadow with the first sunbeams bouncing off the roof, a blue house. Across the street a boy sliding a cylinder of gas over the doorstep, moving stiffly, as if he'd been stuck to the ground with super-glue. There were wrought-iron grilles over the shuttered windows. It was a two-storey house, but Lamarat already knew that from the photograph his father was holding in his hand at that very moment. One small step for a contractor – how many had he already built in Al Homey: a hundred, a thousand, ten thousand? – but a giant step for his father – how much had he paid the contractor: a hundred thousand, a million, a billion inflation-ridden dirhams?

The father was the first to get out of the car, followed by Lamarat and then the sister and the mother (Grandpa had somehow cleverly avoided the count). Their eyes, their backs and their feet moved from left to right and from top to bottom. Sister made a demonstrative show of kicking her right foot against the pale pink step. Halfway between ground and step her foot hung in the air and seemed to hesitate so that it looked like she was in slow motion.

'The house is built on five pillars.'

'I know,' Father said, 'they had to add an extra one since the ground wasn't hard enough everywhere.'

'Yeah, that's kinda what they told me. So now there's a fifth pillar in the middle of the house.'

'I already knew that,' said the bewildered father. 'So what are you trying to tell me, Pa?'

The grandfather adjusted his jellaba and walked over to the heavy metal front door. 'For some strange reason the mosaics are falling off and the paint's started to peel. God knows why.'

As Grandpa spoke, the door slowly opened.

It was Grandma who opened the door.

The taxi driver nodded.

It can begin

That beautiful house lying so innocently in the shadow –
there's something about that house. Take a good look at
it, from top to bottom. Now, at this very moment, the
cement in the nooks and crannies is crumbling like mad.
Damp is creeping up the walls, crackles of lightning are
spreading over the plaster ceilings and the floor tiles are
starting to disintegrate. The house is about to be taken
over by fissures and cracks.

Don't get upset, Father: hire people, let them fix up
the place before there's nothing left to fix because it's
collapsed of its own accord. It's mouldering, crumbling to
pieces at a rapid rate. And nobody's doing a thing;
nobody *can* do a thing. The grandfather and grand-
mother, are they doing anything? No, they're sleeping
through the silent ruin. The fifth pillar in the house – was
it the first to be built or the last? Only Mosa knows. But
the paint is peeling, it's falling off in flakes, faster all the
time. The foundation wasn't laid properly, the water
pipes give off copper, and the chipboard in the kitchen is
infested with woodworm. For a few weeks a year the
Minar family lives in a house that's eating itself up, and
nobody seems to have noticed. Except one person . . .
and Grandpa a bit. Mosa, you rascal, where have you
gone? I'm here, I'm here in the village by the sea; it's cool
here, seventy-two degrees, and there's a gentle breeze. Are

you guys coming? Oh, you mean the house, you want to know what's happening to the house. Ah yes, well, concrete decays, you know, especially in these parts, and there's nothing you can do about it, but what the hell, roses are red, houses are blue, nothing lasts, but I love you. Oh by the way, I saw your boat arrive. It was night, but at the back of the house, by the cactuses, I saw it steaming this way and I knew you guys were on it. Then suddenly I remembered the money. The money for the house, all that money . . . Well, I get mixed up sometimes, and everybody cheats on the exchange rates, even me, especially me. But anyway, we've got other things on our mind right now. Like the wedding, the wedding, and the wedding.

And while Mosa sat by himself and smoked a cigarette in Touarirt, there was great joy in the house in Al Homey that evening: they were home. 'Sit down, sit down,' Grandma said as she herded them into the tiny living room off the kitchen. A plastic rug and cushions had been spread out over the floor. Lamarat, laughing at his own words, later said to his sister, who had spent most of the evening in a daze staring up at the ceiling as if she'd been struck by a bullet, 'That Grandma, what a cutie she is, all I have to do is look at her and she laughs. But the really stupid part is that her little froggie laugh sets me off again, so that I don't even know why I started laughing in the first place.'

The taxi driver nodded. 'Have you ever heard of my mother?' he asked while he slowed down for a hill. 'My mother is a fortune teller.'

'One tellingly without a fortune, I bet,' said the boy. 'So what does she fortune tell?'

'Oh, the usual – the future. She predicts your future, our future, the future of anyone willing to fork out a few dirhams.'

'And how does she do it, predict people's futures, I mean?' The boy's curiosity had been aroused – he was sure it involved blood and sacrificial sheep.

'I don't know exactly, but what she did in my case was to dig a couple of stones out of the cactus field, heat them in a clay pot filled with charcoal – in the meantime I was supposed to sit in a chair and keep quiet – and then she poured water into a pan, fiddled around with the stones in the pot, held the pan of water over my head . . .'

The driver was about to go on, but the boy cut him off mid-sentence, 'I know, I know, they did the same thing to me the last time I was here. They dump the stones in the pan of water and when the ashes come floating to the surface, they see your whole future laid out before them.'

'That's it exactly,' said the driver with a smile.

'And what did your future look like?' asked Lamarat. 'Or do you even know what it looks like? Those old biddies just played around with their stones and didn't tell me a darned thing. They mumbled a bit, and that was that.'

'Yeah, they don't usually let you in on the secret. My mother didn't want to either. She just pinched my cheek . . .'

. . . And they kiss everyone in sight. Those family greetings are purely a formality, you know. First the hugs, the feel of lips on your neck. How many kisses should you give? On what part of the body? Two, three, four, five, six. What to say? Let them do the talking. At any rate that was Rebekka's tactic. Very crafty. Don't resist, let nature take its course. Like the bamboo swaying in the wind's passionate embrace. (The bamboo in the parched soil that was whizzing by Lamarat's window.) She opened her arms to receive the grandmother and let herself be carried along on the tide of words. 'May God watch over you (one kiss), may God take you to His bosom (second kiss), may God look after you (third kiss), may God protect you (fourth kiss), my daughter (fifth kiss), may God have mercy on your children (sixth kiss).' Enough piousness to last into the fourth generation. And sister answered every pronouncement with one of her own: she puckered her lips, kissed her grandmother and appeared to be saying something along the same lines. But if you ask me she simply said the first thing that came into her head, such as, 'Donald Duck (first kiss), sat on a truck (second kiss), crack went the truck (third kiss), bye-bye Donald Duck (fourth kiss). The fifth and sixth kisses were taken up by the refrain of some obscure number from the Eurovision Song Contest. Then Grandma turned to the boy and grabbed him by the waist. He kept his hands behind his back and said nothing, surrendering himself like a limp squid.

They sat down in the living room. A couple of blankets and cushions had been spread out on the floor, but other than that the room was empty. It was pretty depressing. Or as their next-door neighbour in Sesame Seed City would have put it, 'Not exactly my idea of cosy.'

The boy quickly took a seat across from his grand-father, who was sitting all scrunched up with his legs out in front of him. There was a deep, pointy imprint on the ball of his foot. As if it had been stabbed with an ice pick. The soles of his feet were covered with a thick, hard, yellowish layer of skin, like a tumour that had metasta-sized everywhere except at that one point. Actually, it looked more like a star, a dot with lines radiating outward and carving deep gullies in the thick callous.

The dot was a childhood memory, a souvenir of the shoes he'd worn when he was a little boy. The Spanish shoemakers in Melilliar used to sell sandals made out of rubber tyres. The strips of rubber would be held together by a bunch of rusty nails. When the grandfather put them on, the combination of rubber and heat would make his feet sweat. The nails hadn't been pounded in very well – to be honest, they'd just been given a clumsy whack – and some of them stuck out a bit. So as the grandfather was walking back to his village, back to 'The Wolf's Den', one of those cheap two-bit nails pressed itself into his foot. It didn't hurt – walking barefoot hurt a lot more, especially when you were picking prickly pears – but the nail had bored its way through the skin and started to bleed. He left a trail of blood from one village to the next.

Lamarat kept peeking at the scar, while his grandfather busied himself with the latest weather report from Europe. If there was one thing that man was an expert on, it was the state of the weather.

When they had first entered the living room in the new house, the boy's grandmother had pinched his cheek so that he had briefly felt her sticky fingers on his flesh. Her happiness and sticky fingers were due to the fact that her family had come, after ten years, to celebrate a wedding. While Lamarat seated himself next to the grandfather, she chided the father, 'There's no need to be such a tightwad, my son.' He looked at her in surprise and then glared, as if to say: I'm a grown man, Mother, you can't boss me around anymore. 'After all,' she continued, 'your brother is never going to have another wedding, and besides, he helped build this house.' And that was the end of that. Grandma was still the same, an outspoken old dame. And as chatty as ever. To Lamarat too. She had kissed him to death with words – commenting on his height, how he'd got so tall, his physical condition, how he needed to keep eating the right food and not just margarine, how he was going to be the next one to get married. It suddenly occurred to Lamarat that these references to marriage weren't new: the topic had come up a lot during the last holiday. He had been young, too young even to have an ejaculation but that hadn't stopped his grandmother from talking about marriage and the finest quality of henna that she'd prepare, just for him, her darling boy. It might have been better, it occurred to the boy – things were occurring to him left and right – if she hadn't rattled on and on about wet henna and eggs but had told him about the birds and bees instead. That's what she should have done. But perhaps all that talk about marriage and a beautiful girl was a veiled form of sex education. Anyway, Lamarat had always responded to his grandmother's teasing with laughter and evasion. He'd say that he wasn't thinking about getting married, or that you wouldn't catch him letting someone smear his hands with henna or any of that gunk. He wasn't a girl, he wasn't his sister or his mother or his grandmother, whose hands were routinely covered with spickles and dots. Grandma would laugh, nod and trot off to fry him another egg. Or at any rate to do something. The funny thing was that just then, in the living room, after Lamarat had replied, 'I'm not thinking about getting married yet, Grandma,' and was about to launch into a story or a joke to mask his discomfort, Grandma looked at the father and mother and shook her head. 'What's that he's saying, my son, I don't understand.' Father and mother laughed uneasily (when in doubt, grin it out). Grandma said, in an effort to reassure Lamarat, 'When the time is ripe, and eventually it will be, time itself will see to it that he gets the girl he wants.' But she hadn't understood – he'd meant something completely different. For a moment Lamarat felt like he was the illiterate in the family. Which at that moment he was. They might as well have taken a Stanley knife, carved a hole in the parquet of his soul and tossed it in the fire.

Lamarat stood up when he heard his grandmother's

twitters and watched his sister pucker her lips and warble
Norway's entry to the Eurovision Song Contest; Rebekka
swayed in the wind, lived to tell the tale, and would later
bear many children, show them off in the living room,
and live a life of oblivion. Lamarat stood up (I haven't got
a clue as to his future, but bear with me) and walked out
of the living room to inspect the rest of the house.

They were spacious rooms, decorated with mosaics and
gleaming brown geometric tiles. Lamarat had started to
tell the taxi driver about the shower and the cockroaches
that had taken up lodgings around the rim of the Turkish
toilet; how they could also be found on the ceiling, in the
cupboard next to the mothballs, under the night table,
under the bed, in fact everywhere, as if their presence was
some kind of sign. But he got stuck on the subject of his
grandmother, who had spent the rest of the evening
yakking away in the living room. Some people's lives
revolve around zits on their upper lips, others get hung up
on pilgrimages but Grandma lived for her vocal cords. To
her, every one of her words was a sign that she was still
alive; to the boy they were an assault on his ears. She
talked about everything under the sun: the price of eggs,
the size of watermelons, her wish to move back to the
village . . . 'But', the father said after she'd repeatedly
broached the subject at lunch – fish, potatoes swimming
in gravy, hot peppers, melon, all washed down with Coke
or Fanta Florida – 'you were the one dying to move here,
Mother, you've been living the life of Riley here, what's
there for you to do in the village, no listen to me, Mother,
there's nothing left for you in Touarirt, and besides, who
else could take care of this house, who else would mop the
floors and tiles and make sure burglars can't break in and
thieves can't steal? You've been a big help to me so far,
but I'd appreciate it even more if you stayed for a long,
long time.' Having said his piece, the father helped

himself to another slice of watermelon, and the grandfather put a stop to his wife's homesick routine by punctuating sonny boy's speech with an *inshallah*. But she still wanted to go back to her village; if it had been up to her, she'd have gone back with her son, right after the carpenters finished the house with the five pillars.

Lamarat understood a lot of things, for example why someone would become a taxi driver or why Grandma longed for Iwojen, but why the uncle was so anxious to go back to Touarirt was a total mystery to him.

They'd stayed in the village the last time they'd been on holiday. Anyone coming from Melilliar, and there were fewer and fewer of such people, had to pass through various small villages, over a narrow paved road that wound its way into the woods and came out again on the other side of the cape. The village was about three miles from the road. There was no electricity, no running water and no gas. When night fell and the empty platters had been washed and put away, they would sit in the courtyard and Lamarat would scan the sky in search of stars. He stayed awake as long as he could and only went to bed when his uncle did. The next morning he would get up, walk behind the house to the cactus field, do his business, look for a smooth stone – or rather you hoped to god you'd find a smooth stone without any shit or other surprises on it – and look at the sea from behind the cactuses, to see how the sea was doing, to see what mood it was in – preferably calm with a few rimples, like the skin of an elephant that had just got out of bed as well, because then his uncle would be more inclined to go with him. Inside, his breakfast would be waiting for him: an omelette unlike any other omelette he'd ever eaten; and Grandpa would make the tea by boiling a big kettle of water over the fire, pouring the water into the teapot and mixing it with mint leaves and sugar. So much sugar that it always made the boy's jaw drop. It seemed like the couscous spoon would never stop dipping into the bag, seven or eight heaped spoonfuls, but then it was a really good-tasting kind of sugar.

It was during this holiday that the father began to talk about houses being built in cities. In the end it would turn out to be a house in a city uglified by urban sprawl. But, Lamarat asked himself, way out there in the *remrach*, what did they expect of a house whose owners lived in it only six weeks a year? No, Father had bigger plans. Soon. How soon is soon? Is that the sun or the moon, Father? 'Soon, when you kids are married, you'll each have a floor to yourself. You on the top floor, and sister and her husband on the bottom floor.' You should have seen the way he looked when he said that, the way he avoided the sister's eyes, that morning in the courtyard of the house by the sea, where he was sitting with Rebekka and Lamarat. Midi 1 was blaring from a transistor radio and some French guy was saying that some other French guy had won that day in the Tour de France and that he'd been simply fan-tas-tic: pumping madly, attacking the Pyrenees like a pit-bull, zipping along at a mighty speed, what a devastating force was being demonstrated today on the slopes of god-knows-what-mountain! This was followed by the news in the vulgate of the local population. Then the uncle had said, 'Let me make you a proposition, brother, and I think you know what I'm about to say: I'm prepared to guard your house against burglars, I can cash all the cheques that come in and use the money to buy cement and bricks and that kind of stuff, I'll do whatever needs to be done, my dear brother, if you'll help me with something . . . something that'll help me get ahead too . . .' But his sentence had stopped at that crucial point, had been left dangling by those intriguing dots.

What thing? Do what? Did he want a room in the house too? Lamarat didn't know what he was talking about.

The one who knew exactly what he was talking about was his brother. As if he'd been waiting for those very words, he rose up from his cushion and said, 'Don't worry, brother, I'll take care of it, there's no need for you to worry too much.' Actually (and I don't know why it's taken me so long to figure it out since it wasn't that hard), this was the beginning of the wedding. In return for the uncle's services, the father agreed to sail him over to Europe – Rebekka would be his oar.

A simple trade, though the house would get the better part of the bargain. Never before had a Moroccan from Iwojen worked so hard for his brother as the uncle did. After the first cheque arrived he set off for the city, sleeping in a tent next to the man-made crater, next to the mounds of dirt excavated for the pillars on which the house was to be built – a total of five. As the building progressed from frame to every man's castle, he began to sleep in the house, in an improvised lean-to. One day the uncle looked at the house and realized that a turning point had been reached: at this stage you could transform it into either a house or a mosque, a bazaar or a jail. It's just that one of them needs more cement than the other.

The house grew – more cement, more bricks and more paycheques, and along with it Mosa's conviction that before long he'd be living there with *her*.

He saw her for the first time the year before the wedding, the year the house was finished. The parents came over especially for the occasion; the father, tagging along with the uncle to admire the uncle's future home, looked at him sternly. 'She probably needs to get used to you, little brother, do you know what I mean? She's eighteen now and next year she'll be nineteen, God willing, so be careful, because as you know, I'm doing you a favour. You were the one who was in such an all-fired hurry, do you know what I'm saying or don't you? If you only knew how many nights she cried, for weeks on end, but that's all over now. She's not really ready for you, so try to be nice, do you know what I'm saying or don't you?'

Of course the uncle knew what he was saying, and he walked around the neighbourhood with her and gradually tried to let his magic wand do the talking for him, to wave it around and let it cast its spell. Then he spun the wheel of fortune round and round with the promise of an ice-cream cone, a kiss and a gold necklace, each of them accompanied by a hug, until she had no choice but to say, 'Yes, but I want to be independent. Yes, but you have to treat me with respect. Yes, but how do I know you aren't lying? Yes, you've got pretty blue eyes and nobody around here has blue eyes. I need to think about it, I might be willing to give it a try, I wish I could tell you my thoughts, I suppose everything will be okay, I cried my eyes out, you know, but I guess it'll all work out, so we might as well give it a whirl.' And after three times sigh, sigh, sigh, she calmed down and spun the wheel one more time: on a cloudless afternoon in Melilliar's municipal park, walking arm in arm between the thorns of grass, she said, 'All right, I'll marry you, and in Touarirt instead of Al Homey. Why not, of course it'll be okay.'

It's on and on it goes

The girl said yes and the uncle was happy, the family was happy and the house seemed to be made even more beautiful with all that happiness – while one blue-glazed tile after another slowly but inevitably began to come unstuck. You'd never guess, from the way the house stood there on the corner, hidden in the shadow, that it was falling apart. Lamarat felt good when he looked at it. *There's No Place Like Home tralalala lalali*, he sang. To his father a house meant that everything was *tralalala lalali*. Lamarat knew that, he could tell by the way the father held his head when he walked through the house and touched every little thing like . . . like . . . damn I don't know how else to say it . . . like he was touching some sacred object. He bowed by the pillars, poked his nose in the kitchen cupboards, sniffed inside, caressed the toilet seat and flicked the light switch on and off a hundred and one times. Went back outside, for the third time that day, walked from one corner of the lot to the other, squatted down and examined the right side of the house from the perspective of a bullfrog, ran his fingers through the dirt, rolled the pebbles around in his palm, rubbed his right hand up and down the grilles, threw the pebbles back down on the dirt. Bug eyes, faint smile and a helluva lot of looking. The mechanism that had been ticking away for years in a little-used corner of his brain apparently came to an abrupt stop at that moment. It had ticked all that time without fail: work for the house, sleep in the house, slave on the house, pay for the house, and once that was done, it would be work from the house, take potshots at the world from the house, go on a pilgrimage from the house, receive your children and their children in the house and, finally, trade the house in for a bigger house . . .

There's no use crying over built houses, and you could tell by looking at the windows, at the paint – light blue – and at the curlicues on the tiles that he certainly hadn't bitten off more house than he could chew. Indeed, there's no place like home. But what was there about the house that made Lamarat not want to live in it?

When they left a week later to go to Iwojen for the wedding, Lamarat took another look at the house, then another, and another – shit, it's not me, it's the house, but *what* exactly? – and yet he still hadn't figured out what his father had been trying to tell him for years: this was the house in which the boy would celebrate his wedding. An option the uncle had passed up.

He who goes in never comes out again; he who goes outside gets shot at from the inside.

After the bridegroom had left Touarirt because he was dying to be with his true love – a woman of the streets who carried a nail file in her handbag – and to kiss her goodbye and au revoir and tell her that even though she was a you-know-what she was nice and sweet and occasionally surly and ask her why she hadn't let him kiss her for the first eight months, he had hailed a cab. After he got in the car ('Hey, Bucket of Bolts Chalid, how ya' doin'?') the first thing he did besides shaking hands and offering Chalid a cigarette was to ask how long they'd known each other. Chalid counted his fingers. One hand, another hand, and another hand plus an index finger: a total of sixteen years. 'Isn't that something,' the bridegroom said, and then he stared wordlessly out the window at the landscape undulating past them. The bridegroom rolled down the window (using his teeth since the handle was broken and he didn't happen to have a spanner on him), stuck his arm outside – cigarette within easy reach – and told the driver that they'd known each other for a very long time. 'Since we were kids, right?'

The driver nodded, changed gears and headed for the forest up ahead.

After they'd entered the forest, pine needles everywhere – 'it smells so good' outsiders usually said – the groom began talking about their shared childhood. 'Do you remember, sure you do, that school we went to over by the Spanish spring? And do you remember the girl who sat in front of us, three desks away, yeah, that's the one, Mimuna, the daughter of that old humpbacked Azeboch, who made her wear a scarf, except that she'd take it off the minute she got behind the hills at the back of the house, and who could blame her: a beautiful head of hair, gleaming like fresh suet, all the way to the roots . . . Have you ever seen anyone since then with more beautiful hair, tell me honestly, ¿*compadre* . . . ?' (Sometimes the bridegroom thought up names for his friends, right there on the spot, for no reason at all.) 'I was so happy when she came to school: her hair, her *everything* was perfect . . . but to tell you the truth I wasn't crazy about her . . .'

'That's news to me,' the driver said, 'why the sudden change?'

'I made a recent discovery. Not one single girl interests me. Not a one.'

'That's odd,' the *compadre* said. He felt like asking and saying more, but right then the road required his full attention. Lying in wait for him in the forest were seven hairpin bends. And watching and waiting behind each hairpin bend was a future that might very well include the inside of a full gut splattered on someone else's windscreen. To avoid such a grisly end you have to abide by the following rules:

1. Reduce your speed fifty yards before the curve (experienced cabbies cut it down to twenty-five or thirty yards, but since he didn't believe in such a thing as experience, Chalid stuck to fifty).
2. Honk the horn ten yards before the curve (at least three-times).
3. Take the curve at a snail's pace.
4. Accelerate after the curve, except when there's another curve coming up.

'You know what,' said the groom once the curves were behind them, 'all those girls that you and I used to look at, the girls who came to the spring to fill their *bombats*, the girls in our class, the girls we knew from the other villages in Iwojen, the girls we worked our way through at weddings, all those girls I claimed I was in love with, that I'd die for, the girls in Melilliar, the handful of kooks in Al Homey, the masses I'm trying to block out, the hordes being chomped up by my brain, all those girls flashed through my mind a couple of days ago, when I was fiddling around in the courtyard. It gave me a funny feeling, seeing all their faces again. There were too many of them, you know. You of all people must know how many I've had.'

This the driver could readily agree with. The bride-groom-to-be had indeed had many. Never enough, of course – why else do sultans have harems – but just enough so he could look back with a certain amount of undisguised pride. Weddings in Iwojen were a treasure trove of female flesh. Sometimes Chalid would drive around Iwojen for no particular reason. And some of those times he'd run into girls he'd fooled around with at weddings, now lingering outside the high walls of their husband's houses, going shopping, heading for the spring. Girls he'd picked up at weddings by cocking his eye and his hips, now in the role of wife – some with children, but all with their own donkey and a pair of *bombats*. The very same girls who'd come to the weddings with their mothers and, while their fathers were inside praying with their beads, would sit in the courtyard and watch the women mix the henna that was to be smeared on the hands of the bride and groom, who would then press their hands against the wall of the bridal chamber. However, the girls were much more interested in the boys who kept wandering into the courtyard one by one in search of food. Besides, the girls had been ordered, by the groom himself, to stay outside: their place was where the music was.

'And the best part about the girls', chortled Mosa, 'is that later in the evening, when the bride and groom were making their handprints on the wall, the girls would slip away from their mothers who were too busy chanting prayers and rejoicing to notice, and go behind the house with us for a quickie.' The bridegroom laughed. 'But there I was, poking around in the courtyard, and I remembered the thighs of every girl I'd ever poked. And it made me sick to my stomach. You know what I mean?'

There were still five miles to go before they reached the border town of F. The driver shifted into third and took the first of the four hills between the forest and F. You jerk, thought Chalid. A taxi driver is the last person who'd understand.

*

The prospective bridegroom touched the seat.

'Upholstery's still good.'

'Yeah, a Mercedes,' said the driver.

'You been to Lolita's lately?' Mosa asked with a leer.

'Nah, Mosa, I haven't been there in ages.'

'Okay, that's cool, but let me tell you, now that we're on the subject, last night I sat there in the courtyard and tried to count the number of breasts I've fondled in Lolita's. I think of every one of them as my personal possessions. God, how many breasts do you suppose I've fondled? Count 'em, Chalid: one hundred, two hundred, maybe a hundred thousand. Do you know what I mean or don't you? It's impossible to count 'em, because I've tweaked so many. Did it hurt? Nah, course not, it felt good to fondle them, to be a man. God, the tricks we used to use, wondering how long they'd stay firm, do you know what I'm saying or don't you, *sidi compadre* Chalid? Soon I'm going to have only one woman. After tonight I'll have only one pair of breasts to feast my hands on. What'll it be like? You think I'll get depressed? Say something, Chalid, you always have a fitting answer for everything. Say a comforting word that'll at least help me get to sleep. Hey Chalid, my friend, are you as hung up on Lolita's as I am?'

If there was one thing the driver knew about himself, it was that he would never again set foot in Lolita's Bar in Melilliar, the one by the municipal park, open to anyone with enough courage between his legs, the bar next to the public phone booths from which the uncle would call his girl – 'I love you, baby, and thank god it's not raining here in Melilliar' – and do his best to give her an answer whenever she asked how much longer, baby, how much longer? That changed. First it was a year, then only eight months, then six, then five, then it went fast, four, three, two, one, zero zip zilch, see ya' soon and say hi to that crazy brother of yours. Eighteen or twenty times that year the uncle had hung up the phone and made use of the occasion – he was in the neighbourhood anyway – to go to confession at Lolita's.

Lolita's Bar couldn't have been more than fifteen feet by fifteen feet or maybe ten by ten or twenty by twenty, Chalid didn't know for sure, since to him it was sometimes only one woman wide. But one thing he did know was that Lolita's had ten times ten bottles of various liquids along the back wall and that the booze and the babes cost four times your weekly salary. And all that for a couple of minutes – admit it, Mosa, you couldn't hold back much longer – of fickie-fick.

Chalid didn't fickie-fick at Lolita's anymore because he'd been so put off by something that had happened to him there that he didn't think he'd ever be able to enjoy himself in that place again. He talked about it openly. It was the kind of thing your friends like to tease you about – 'Hey, what's happening, Chalid, you suddenly turn into a faggot or something, what you gotta realize is that those tarts are all like that' – the kind of thing you wish hadn't happened, but then these things happen because they're supposed to, if you know what I mean. 'But why should I listen to you?' the driver would sometimes lash out in the café The Gimp had stopped coming to long ago. 'If you guys had ever seen her the way she really is, you'd be wishing your balls would fall off too.'

'Man, you must've been smoking something that day. You're hallucinating, you're sick, crazy, god knows what. Anyway, who are you? Just an ordinary taxi driver. Not somebody you have to believe.'

Any normal person would have reacted to an insult like that, but Chalid didn't seem to have heard. Staring meditatively into space, he continued calmly, 'If only you guys had seen her. But what the hell am I saying, you've all seen her. God only knows how many guys have humped her, what with those gorgeous earrings, smooth eyebrows, long eyelashes and red lips, just right, and of course they're even more beautiful when you're drunk, do you know what I'm saying or don't you? Humph, they turn up their noses at Heineken, so you give 'em Amstel or wine 'cause it's so fine, ha ha ha, that's a laugh, since when do women have any taste! Except when they're drunk, then you'd be surprised to hear how much they see. I danced with her, to the song that goes: *You're as beautiful as a sunflower, so I'm wondering why you picked me?* She took me to Lolita's Hotel, not far from Lolita's Bar. Ten minutes to walk there, one minute to pay a thousand pesetas, two minutes to get to the room. Five minutes for a bit of cuddling – you gotta give a woman like that the idea that she's special, otherwise there's no challenge. Two minutes to get undressed, etc., etc. We lay down on the bed, and I felt like my dick was in the hands of an angel. There was only one thing I wanted now, and that was the she-devil who was reeling from one side of the room to the other. 'Hurry up,' I begged her, 'I'm one giant throb.'

'And then, believe it or not, it was like I was seeing a mirage. The she-devil began to strip, and with every layer that came off I got a better look at the real her. She removed more than she should have. If The Gimp was here, I'm sure he'd say, 'That's what you get for trying to make your dreams come true. You win some and you lose some, by which I mean that you had a bad roll with a bad dice and you got a bad shock, but you brought it all down on yourself, *ulla pulla*.' But you guys haven't said a word. That's because you're still young. May God protect you from such a humiliation.

'First she took off her dress, her pink tank top, her bra and her panties. Then her fingernails. No problem, I could handle that – floozies always wear fake nails, or else they wouldn't be floozies. After that she fished a tissue out of her bag and wiped off a thick layer of red lipstick. Then, using her thumb and forefinger, she peeled off her false eyelashes, first her left eye and then her right eye. That was followed by her earrings, her high heels, a dab of mascara near her nose, and finally her wig. Then, I'd better stop now or I'll rip her heart out, she started to take out her dentures – she picked up a glass and was heading for the bathroom with her fingers fumbling at her mouth. Do you understand what I'm trying to say, guys? I've seen the light, I'm converting to a life of solitude.'

The driver had also told this story to his old buddy, who had listened but ignored his advice. On the contrary, Mosa's visits to the girls in Melilliar became even more frequent. Because he was addicted to fairytales. Mosa was the kind of person who, in other parts of the world, would have been referred to as an idealist.

He was the kind of guy who believed that a pussy tasted like honey. Or rather did until the day, he was eighteen at the time, he'd landed his umpteenth girl in Lolita's and later that evening, just to try it out, had pressed his lips to one of those juicy beavers. All it took was the pressure of two thighs and the ideal on which he'd hoped to feast, to buzz around like a bee in a honeycomb, had been sent to storybook land forever.

Later on the bridegroom would joke about what had happened. And yet he was sure that somewhere on this planet there was a woman who really did taste like butter and honey melted over a smouldering fire, a delicacy his mother used to make for him on special occasions.

So it was extra interesting that less than a year before he skipped out on his wedding, he'd come to the taxi driver to tell him that he'd finally found her, that he'd met her when she came to Al Homey. 'We went for a walk in the municipal park in Melilliar; she put her arm through mine, and we strolled around arm in arm, like film stars.' After that first encounter, he'd waited in F., where you have to change cabs, until his friend the taxi driver showed up. He'd thrown his arms around his neck – hey, what's happening, the driver had thought – and had whispered into his ear that he was in love. 'This is really *it*, you know. She's my ticket outta this one-horse town.'

Mosa was the kind of person who made no secret of his personal suffering. He reported that she came from Sesame Seed City (!) – it was the first thing he said – and that she was as beautiful as a gold bracelet, or even better, as beautiful as the diamonds in the display windows of the jewellery shops, the ones that took up two entire blocks of a shopping area a few blocks west of downtown Al Homey. And in one of those shops he was going to buy his girl a gold necklace, a diadem and a pair of earrings. Plus one of those copper-coloured bands that you cinch around your waist, which cost ten million Moroccan francs, bracelets that'd set you back a million francs a piece, and diamond earrings to the tune of half a million francs per earring. The driver had laughed and remembered that Mosa didn't have two francs to rub together. Had there been a church in Iwojen, Mosa would have been known as a churchmouse. But money wasn't important, was it? He loved her, with all his heart, not to mention his liver and spleen; and he'd care for her, the way a farmer cares for his onion plot. Mosa had never been in such a joyful, expectant mood. 'She fell for me because I looked like someone from the north.' That was true – he was white, alabaster white, which is why he was called The Mosque Worm. Not so much because he never set foot in a mosque, but because his skin didn't even have enough pigment for a tan. That's why Mosa, unlike most of the people in Iwojen, was not drawn to the sea. He only went there when he had to, for example, to please his visiting nephew, a chubby little kid who wanted to see the sea and wouldn't take no for an answer. So Mosa had clambered down the endless slopes with him, trudged through the sand and even briefly dipped his toes in the water while the nephew was undressing, but the sea itself *had never sipped even one drop of sweat from his body.* He preferred to take refuge in the shadow of a boulder and listen to a transistor radio that brought the news and Oum Kalsoum from Egypt. Mosa, the handsome young man blessed with the appearance of an *aromi*, a Westerner, was also the only one who could pass through the Spanish customs in Melilliar without having to show his identity papers.

Ilovemybeer

He's back and has been taken to the village by the sea. Welcome, welcome, and the highest praise and honour to the one who apprehended the fugitive bridegroom and returned him to his native soil.

'Where I found him? I tailed him to this hotel. He went in and I . . . well, I hung around the door, waiting. Some guy came along and asked me if I'd do it for a thousand pesetas. I said no and waited for Mosa to come out again. But he went back to Lolita's and only came out when they threw him out – giggling, arms hanging, staggering all over the place. I finally went into action. 'My dear uncle,' I said, 'today's the big day, ya' know, the wedding, ya' know, the fleshpots can wait, ya' know. Will you come with me . . . please?' He was so drunk it was like a blind man being led by a seeing-eye dog. And the whole time he kept saying over and over, 'Ilovemybeer, Ilovemybeer.' Not in a normal voice, no, but in a high-pitched giggle with an occasional low note in three-quarter time: 'I-lovemy-beer, I-lovemy-beer . . .' and that's how we spent the time waiting for a taxi that would hopefully take us back to Touarirt as quickly as possible.'

He went through customs with the gentleman in question – the tangible evidence that his search had not been in vain – on his back. The first to see him exit the customs office was Chalid, sitting in the shade of a thin, leafless, lifeless tree. Was it really him, with a Marlboro in his left hand and his right hand swathed in a thick bandage that looked like pink toilet paper? (In Iwojen toilet paper is sold in small roadside stores. There's a brand called El Hilal; there's also an all-female band called El Hilal: Berber music on video-cassette.) At that moment the thermometer in Chalid's cab pointed to seventy degrees. And that was a vast improvement over the hellish temperature in which Lamarat had been driven to F.

The boy, who felt beds of sweat hopscotching down his body, got into the car and tried to shut the door, but it wouldn't shut. 'Just a sec,' said Chalid. The driver of the 1978 Mercedes 240D chucked his cigarette under another taxi that was also waiting for the last customers from the crown colony. The houses by the border town, up on the hills and on the road to Al Homey, had all closed their shutters. A group of dark-skinned men were sitting on a wall near the taxi stand, presumably Nigerians. (Or were they Gambians or Ghanaians or other people who, like the inhabitants of Iwojen, especially the taxi driver, were crazy about soup made out of sheep heads? Iranians were also sheep-head aficionados, preferring to eat them with the eyes still in the head.) The blacks, seated in lawn chairs, were holding bowls with various pointy bones jutting out of them and dripping with a blood-red sauce – soup stock mixed with *semoule de blé dur*, otherwise known as durham-wheat semolina. They'd pick up a piece with their fingers, chew it down to the bone, suck out the brains and eat the head-cheese. The entire evening had been spent eating. Lamarat had noticed them stuffing their faces the moment he'd passed through customs. He immediately recognized the bones and all that picking and gnawing as a wrestle with sheep heads. His mother had once fixed half a sheep head for him; it had a strong, sweet taste. The next time you eat a sheep head you should think of the queen – Lamarat had once hacked two hundred sheep heads in half for her. Of course the queen didn't know that he'd slaved away like that – only Lamarat knew.

It happened like this: one of the more memorable days in Lamarat's life had been spent in a butcher shop. Okay, granted, the whole thing took place in a dream, but then how can we explain the fact that Lamarat woke up bathed in sweat, with sore arms, a head that felt like it had been hacked in two and the feeling that he'd just quit his job? In the dream a day lasted ten hours, from eight in the morning to six at night, and not a second longer. Through some unhappy coincidence Lamarat wound up being in the dream on the busiest possible day. 'Here, grab this,' said his employer, a fat man with dandruff on his shoulders, a greasy pimp's moustache, and the arms of a gorilla, and he started throwing him bag after bag of sheep heads. Where am I, thought Lamarat, oh yeah, now I remember, it's all right: I'm in downtown Sesame Seed City and people with dark skins are walking by the windows and peering in, hoping to find a tasty titbit to put in their *semoule de blé dur*. But wait, that didn't make sense, because first of all it wasn't cold outside, but blazing hot, almost as hot as in Chalid's cab, and secondly, the street was filled with white people, honest-to-goodness whites who'd been brought in from the northern part of the country to populate Lamarat's dream. The butcher didn't mince his words. 'Work hard and do your job right, 'cause there are hordes of blacks outside who have got their eye on you, do you know what I mean or don't you?' And he shoved another bag into his arms. There seemed to be no end to the stream of plastic bags. There was a stack of them, at least six foot high, on the white tiles with the black grouting. While he worked,

Lamarat silently mimicked the owner, '. . . do you know what I mean or don't you, do you know what I mean or don't you . . . ?'

But it wasn't a dream – to prove it there was a third person in the shop, a man called Van Splat, whom the black whites outside knew all too well. This gentleman had been commissioned by Her Royal Highness, the Queen of Ollanda, herself. There was no end to the dream of words pouring down on the heads of the Chinese outside (that's how crowded it was – there must have been at least a billion of 'em). Some of the Chinese whipped into the shop to ask for an income-tax form. 'How often do I have to tell you I won't be a party to such tricks,' the boss shrieked, 'we leave jokes like that to the government, that wretched government that takes you for every penny you've got so you can't even feel around in your pocket and think, whooee, I've got money to burn. Do you know what I mean, ping-pong, tik-tak, slim pickings here. Buzz off, go celebrate New Year, dammit! Here we are in the middle of summer and you guys are celebrating the year of the fatted BSE calf, unbelievable! How come you guys don't eat sheep heads?'

'Boss,' asked Lamarat in real life, 'why do you sell only sheep heads? Why not Wiener schnitzels, codfish, mercurochrome or, for all I care, income-tax forms. I mean, why just these bloody skulls?'

'You ungrateful dog!' The butcher snatched up another bag and spat out the words so hard that the boy had to wipe his cheek with his shirt cuff. 'Don't you understand anything, what is it with you damn kids these days, you don't wash your backsides, you stuff yourself with minced cat paws and you can't even understand why I like to sell sheep heads to the queen.' 'You have no right to talk to me like that,' said Lamarat, but he said it so softly that only the whites outside heard it, and they started clapping – in encouragement – louder and louder, so loud that some of the supporters in the street turned black and had to be resuscitated. There was a momentary blackout, but the stupid dream just kept going on and on. 'Listen up, kid, it's not hard to explain. These sheep heads are the only thing that Her Royal Muckety-Muck eats: she's served one hundred sheep heads every day. I'm told her husband likes 'em too, but we shouldn't be gossiping. She doesn't just eat for the sake of eating. No, the woman's a real gourmet. And who the hell did she choose to be Purveyor to the Royal Household? Me! For as long as I live, her whims are my command. What does she care that I go home smelling like sheep, so that even my own wife calls me lambkin.' 'You know what you ought to do?' said Lamarat. 'You ought to get stupid people to do this work for you, some of those dummies from the audience out there. That's how things have been done for millions of years. I mean, meat is raw, so you invent fire; there are too many people, so you throw them in the fire; there are too many fires, so you open a butcher shop. That'll do the trick: go out and get some people who can do the work and bring them here.' Lamarat and his cockeyed notions were making the butcher more depressed by the minute. So while he placed the heads one by one on the chopping block so that Lamarat could chop them one by one, he said, 'Brains fried with chopped onions, garlic and a pinch of basil, the standard recipe – she can't get enough of it,' which he repeated no less than three times. 'Listen to me, kid, those people out there don't want to smell like sheep. They'd rather eat pork. And you know what they say about pork: it's cheaper and makes better gravy. Besides, those people out there are getting paid a lot of money for what they do.' 'So what *do* they do?' Lamarat asked. 'They make headlines, one after the other, type headlines, hype and hyperbolize, weigh pros and cons, polish and boot, screw and break the ice, dream up fairytales. Look.' The butcher yanked open his overalls. And what do you think the boy saw? A potbellied stomach with a tattoo in horrible gothic swirls: MILK DOES A BODY GOOD. 'Just a few decades ago this rated a big headline. It's absolutely crazy, but they earn good money that way. The funny thing is, it's catching on in other countries, and the people most likely to catch it are those least suited to that kind of work, like taxi drivers.' The man hawked, spat on a hacked-open sheep head and crammed it into a green and yellow bag. 'Gives the sauce an extra flavour, do you know what I mean or don't you?'

Dreams. What are dreams? Primal urges, poor blood circulation, a sweet little man who throws sand in your eyes to lure you into an exciting adventure.

Who the hell knows, Lamarat said to himself in his dream. Just then a bag slipped out of his hands. *A tisket, a tasket, a green and yellow basket, I wrote a letter to my love, and on the way I dropped it.* Right, you drop a hanky here, a hanky there, and then what happens: you run, tap someone on the back and, after the applause dies down, you go home. Over and out. (But in his dream Lamarat kept on running because where was the handkerchief, where was he, where was everyone else?)

'I want you to shut up, speed it up, chop-chop, and stop talking back to your elders.' He's right – it's wrong to shoot off your mouth on the first day. Just then the street outside was emptied of people, in direct proportion to the speed at which the butcher's bags were being filled with sheep heads. And all the while it seemed as if the heads were never going to stop coming. Repetitive work is boring, thought Lamarat, and he turned over again in his bed. With every blow of the axe, bones flew through the air like a bursting fragmentation bomb and scratched the tiles. Blood dribbled down the heads, oozed onto the chopping block, congealed on Lamarat's hands, crept under his nails and spattered on the floor. But it was for a noble cause: he was doing it for the queen. 'Tomorrow she's got guests and she'll be serving heads,' Mr Van Splat said while Lamarat exploded one sheep head after another. 'Not again,' said the butcher. 'Doesn't she like things like vitamin supplements or cashew nuts, they'd make a nice change and you know what they say: variety is the spice of life.' With these cheerful words the butcher handed over the heads plus the bill addressed to Her Royal Highness, though she would never get to see it because the man who came to pay would wad it up into a ball the minute he left the shop and throw it into the gutter. 'Bye-bye, so long,' the butcher said to Van Splat, 'give her my regards, bon appetit, whatever – I never know what to say.' So after that distinguished gentleman left, a couple of Nigerians came in and asked for exactly that amount: a couple of heads. The butcher gave them short shrift. Meanwhile, as Lamarat scraped the congealed blood from his hands, he decided it was time to chuck the whole thing. He took off his apron and told the boss to go find somebody else. At that very moment, just as he quit his job, six o'clock on the dot, Lamarat slammed the door of his dream shut and woke up.

In the butcher shop he had walked away from there had been two lawn chairs. On the patio next to the café most of the people were sitting on lawn chairs. Several men from the border town of F. were grouped around the door, chugging tea, coffee and soda, also sitting on lawn chairs. The driver used to pop into the café from time to time, but recently he'd been going more often because their wobbly wood and metal chairs (made in Algeria) had been replaced by plastic lawn chairs. And those lawn chairs were occupied by dark-skinned men who had travelled a long way so that they could cross over to countries where they could become salesmen. What they had to sell was themselves, their services as asbestos removers, belt peddlers, hawkers of women's underwear or track suits or cartons of cigarettes (Casawinstonbest) from the Czech Republic, as display dummies (live dolls strutting their stuff behind a plate of glass – drool and tap the glass with marbles), as dancers, purse-snatchers, baseball-bat vendors, doormen, as anything you can think of (except of course headline-makers). The driver of the Mercedes Benz 240D (imported from Belgium) knew a story about a thumbtack salesman who had left behind the hovels and dirt floors of his homeland in hopes of a better life in another country. And what did he find there? A mirror image of himself, now in possession of fancy shoes and fancy ideas, but living in another hovel. His job? Pretzel salesman. In fact a very large number of people left a very large and very poor country to sell thumbtacks and cream puffs somewhere else – thumbtacks because they were useful and cream puffs because pretty girls like to eat them, especially when they're filled with whipped cream. Exactly, thought Bucket of Bolts Chalid in the taxi. Mosa (who burped and muttered 'I love my beer') is like all the others: off to seek his fortune, off to seek dozens of girls. But why should Mohammed go to the mountain if the mountain will come to Mohammed? Tax-free and in handy cling-wrap. I mean, take a look around and what do you see? Satellite dishes, accordion shutters, Pepsi ads, beltless maxi-skirts, Ilikeyou make-up, and chocolate ice cream instead of tuna on French bread. Nothing new under the sun.

I don't understand people like that, Chalid realized, I

don't understand people who leave hearth and home so they can be the same . . . somewhere else.

Lamarat, his uncle glued to his side, waved to Chalid, what's-his-name.

To refresh your memory: my name is Chalid and I come from a village up above yours, high up on the hillside where the soil is red, and you, two-timing Iwojenian, don't you come from down below, where the water flows, where everything's so green? And in places where there's no water – don't you have worn-out tyres and rusty tins of yeast, the ones showing a baker taking bread out of an oven? Isn't there lots of litter in the valleys where erosion is eating away at the hot air? Things like leaky *bombats* and cast-off frying pans? And you, the kid from the north, you were born in a place where the land is able to feed its people, so why did you leave? Oh, I know your father, so there's no need for you to say, 'I wasn't the one who wanted to go.' And there's no point in bringing up all the fame that might have been yours. Your father played a mean game of Parcheesi himself – he played a lot of games on that tiny plot of land of his, down in the valley, between the spring and the pomegranate trees, where he used to grow grapes, onions and potatoes. Onions and grapes can be eaten with bread – bread that your father's mother used to make from yeast she got out of a tin. And the potatoes were always fried in Kristal olive oil. Some-times there was meat to go with the potatoes. I say sometimes, because meat was expensive and not always available. Up on the red soil, on the asphalt road to F., there was a butcher who sold steaming beef liver to the highest bidder. Your father used to go by there occasion-ally on his way home from the mosque. There's nothing better than a good meal and a good shit after prayers. Anyway, he went to the mosque over by the highway, yeah, the one down the road from the blacksmith. Your village used to have its own mosque, did you know that, but your father didn't go to that one. I know for a fact that your mother took you there once. How old were you? About three. First she smeared you with the milk of a white plant that has yellow pollen. This was supposed to ward off evil spirits for the rest of your livelong days. After that she took you to the prayer hall in the deserted mosque and had you perform your first prayer. My, how you cried. You screamed so loud she had to take you out again. And now here you are, twenty years old, wanting to go back to Touarirt, and you're disappointed in your homeland.

There was no one in F., except for the blacks on the benches and in the cafés, who could hear the taxi driver think. He walked over to the car and slammed the door. 'Shuts better from the outside.' The driver wanted to talk to Lamarat about his uncle, about the uncle he'd found. The uncle who'd been bundled into the car, where he stuck his thumb in his mouth and immediately fell asleep.

Snoring loudly, still with his thumb in his mouth, Mosa sat slumped in the back seat. He wasn't a speck of trouble. 'Where on earth did you find him?' Bucket of Bolts Chalid asked. 'In Melilliar, yeah I know that, but Melilliar is big, so where exactly in Melilliar? Try to be a little more specific.'

But what should he tell him? That he'd gone to a certain place in Melilliar, where he'd been surrounded by trees and grass (the grass as hard as steel, like green blades you could use to slice sheep heads in half and gladden the heart of a queen: no splinters, two perfectly equal halves). According to the instructions Lamarat had been given, he should then walk a bit further. ('It's in back of the municipal park, which is by the Spanish plaza. Go

128

through the park, and you'll come to a kiosk, the kind where they sell sweets, Marlboros and ice-cream bars, and voilà, you'll find him there,' Pimple Face had told him while draining his glass of tea. 'It's no big deal.') The uncle had come out of a café, where a neon sign that hadn't flashed in years spelled the name LOLITA. The boy will never forget those unlit letters: L-O-L-I-T-A. (Later, when he was sitting in the bus beside Mosa, who kept jabbing him in the ribs, giggling and turning away, he could no longer form them into a word. All he knew was that that there were six letters, two of which were the same; six letters that kept sloshing around inside his head.) Another thing he'll never forget is the woman the uncle was holding on to, a Lolita girl – and in Lamarat's eyes that was a very big deal.

'Chatischa, Chatischa!' Lamarat had wanted to shout when he caught sight of her and a pair of hands, *his* hands, the fingers calloused from hoeing onions, resting halfway between a fleshy body and – hopefully for the uncle – a willing spirit, exerting pressure on the place where life is made and born, or just above, what difference does it make. Anyway, the boy concluded in a flash, if that's a Lolita bar and she's a Lolita girl, then they must be on their way to a Lolita hotel to get their lolitas off.

But, my dear young man, why didn't you say to the Lolita uncle and his playmate: stop, in the name of love, go back to your soon-to-be wife! Why didn't you leap out and block his way so he couldn't go down the path of sin and iniquity? Hmm, Lamarat thought, hmm, I didn't do that, I didn't say a word, I didn't move a muscle. Actually, I should have done what my pimply cousin suggested: 'If you find him in a café, give him a mournful look, like a dog waiting for a bone, and tell him to come home or something like that – anyway, remember to say it so no one else can hear you, otherwise everybody and his dog will know that your father and your family have suffered a terrible loss of face – if everything's okay he'll go with you.'

'And if it's not okay, if he ignores me? What then, oh all-knowing cousin who makes a killing on cheap caftans and stinky wallets?'

'Then', the Oracle of Al Homey replied, 'you, your pappy and the little bride will be up shit creek. Go now and leave me in peace.' So Lamarat had gone forth and searched, but conquered nothing and no one ('And yet it's damned im*po*rtant, sonny,' the Gimp would have said, 'why can't you get it through your thick skull: winning or losing is the only thing that matters; nobody gives a hoot what the game is or who you play against'), and now he was crawling along in a cab, for all the world like he was paddling through an overdose of shit. And all the while, his head was going ninety miles an hour.

You should have said something, anything. He must have gone and done you-know-what . . . Now that he isn't coming, now that you let him go, what next . . . ? The woman he was with . . . that was the one your cousin was talking about, the one he rushed outside to see . . . You think she does it for money, you think she's any good, you think she'd do it with you, you think you'd want to do it with her . . . ? No, no, I don't want to have thoughts like that, quit tormenting me, you sick brain, you've been reading too many tabloids! *If melting looks were anything to go by, old unc was burning with desire for her . . . Was she wearing nail polish? High heels . . . ? She had on red shoes, didn't she . . . ? And what'd she have in that bulging bag of hers – a towel, a pair of panties, a lubricant . . . ?* It wasn't true, they just went off to talk, he wanted to talk to her, to tell her it was over, that he was going away . . . *You stood there behind that tree and you were shocked, more shocked than you'd ever*

been in your entire life, but you didn't do a blessed thing;
your mother took you to the mosque and it was all for
nothing, your father brought you to Ollanda and it was
all for nothing, he fed you veal cutlets bought you clothes
sent you to Koran school combed your hair and it was all
for nothing do you know what I'm saying or don't you I
mean you grew up and it was all for nothing you might as
well have become a Parcheesi player since at least then
you might have amounted to something in this cockama-
mie life of yours . . .

Nothing plus nothing equals nothing, Lamarat thought.
Turning to Chalid, he said, 'Home James, if you know
what I mean. And step on it.'

A few days before those king-sized blows came crashing
down on Lamarat's head and set off a ticking in
Chalid's head too, a few days before that black day,
Lamarat met a man in Al Homey called Ammunir,
a.k.a. the Gimp.

Ammunir sold detergent and sanitary towels. 'And
remember,' Lamarat's grandmother said when she sent
him to the hole in the wall across the street, 'don't call him
"Gimpy".' Inside the shop, the best Parcheesi player of all
time talked to him about his uncle. In between throws he
also broached the subject of the uncle's hanky-panky.

Ammunir also knew Lamarat's father. 'Your father's a
smooth talker, a real operator. He knew it was wrong to
give her to him, deep down he knew it. Look, there are
only two absolute truths in life: don't do business with
women (and I mean that in more ways than one), and
having a woman on board brings misfortune to a ship.
These are the only two truths. Do you want to know
where I learned them? Take a guess.'

Lamarat guessed and guessed, but still didn't know. 'I
give up, tell me.'

'From the game, from the dice – the more I throw the dice, the more insights I have, the more I play and the less I talk, the happier I am. Look at me: I'm ugly, I know that, even little old ladies take to their heels when they see me. I walk with a limp, I know that too. I couldn't catch up with them even if I wanted to – I had that pounded into me before I could even walk. But I've got something no one else has: I can play the game, and every time I throw the dice another ineradicable truth reveals itself to me.

'People often say to me, "But my dear Ammunir, what you're doing is wrong." My friends tell me that, and then fall from my tree like rotten apples. More and more of them are coming to me with their silky voices and snake eyes: "Games and dice are instruments of the devil; they're not good for you, not good for anybody, so swear you'll stop, Ammunir, it's forbidden by God." "Then I'll find another god," I tell them. "That won't help, Ammunir. No god will allow you to keep niggling and nudging the dice the way you do! Look, Ammunir, you've dug yourself into a hole. All you need now is a bucket of lime. Give it up, you'll be spared a lot of pain." Well, let me tell you, I threw those bastards right out of my shop. "Be gone with you, you pharisees," I shouted at them, "you're gambling with other people's lives. That so-called hocus-pocus *Shitan* of yours is fine with me, because if Parcheesi is an instrument of the *shitan*, then I'm faring well by him, so let me have my devils".' All of his conversation with Lamarat ended in blasphemies like that.

'Let me get back to my dice. Go take a shower or something, you look all sweaty. By the way, my dear Lamarat, son of Minar the Sloppy Dresser, do you pray?'

'No, why do you ask?'

'*Hai*, don't try to fool me, I can see right through you: you don't pray, you've never prayed and even if you've tried to pray, you only thought of it as an experiment.'

'Yeah, I guess.' Lamarat gaped at Ammunir the Converter. 'I never thought of it as an experiment. I learned how to pray at Koran school, of course, and I even gave it a go once or twice after that, but it kind of petered out, if you know what . . .'

'Of course I know what you mean, of course I know, because of the game. The body is subject to erosion, heavy erosion. But cheer up, not all has been lost: trot on in there and try to pray. Drive those snakes out of your body and say *thereisnogodgreaterthanAllah* ten times out loud. Come on, go in there, and make sure you say it loud enough for me to hear.'

Well, if that doesn't take the cake, Lamarat thought. The same guy who calls himself the disciple of the antichrist, our supermonopolist, wants to teach me a lesson. 'If I understand you correctly, you yourself don't do too much praying these days.'

'Humph! I won't stoop to answer an accusation like that. All I can say in my own defence is that I no longer have to pray to anyone. In your case erosion has set in. However, enough seeds can still be sown, something beautiful can still grow, provided you want it to. My case is totally different: my land has been washed away, the subsoil is gone, there's nothing left but a pair of dice and an occasional tin of mangoes. Even little old ladies don't want me, but I've already told you that.'

It was hard not to lose your temper with this apostate, so Lamarat went home and lay down for a nap, and later that afternoon he took a stab at praying – praying to the bountiful God who was greater than the Eiffel Tower, the World Trade Centre and the Seven Wonders of the World all rolled into one; the God who was greater than all understanding of dice and dicely things.

By the way, it didn't work. Halfway through the second

prayer Lamarat began to picture thousands of ways to walk with a limp. This made him laugh so hard that the only way he could get himself to stop was to jam a corner of his prayer rug into his mouth.

As I was saying, everything is fine until you suddenly find yourself confronted with cogs and wheels that are turning the wrong way and developing cracks that no glue in the world can fix; until the sun is so high in the sky that everything withers and dies, food prices skyrocket and people start saying a quick prayer for every little thing. Habits that stick, especially when you can claim in times of prosperity that you owe your well-being to those quick prayers – all the more reason to keep saying them. Superstition, it's called, and why not? The words come to you automatically – Lamarat noticed this all too well in the taxi from F. to Al Homey.

During this part of the trip a family occupied the empty seats. Every time they came to switchback, the husband would relate another crazy episode from his life and punctuate it with a short *bismillah* to the tenth power while the wife would grunt her approval and stuff the edge of her scarf back in her mouth.

'When I lived in Libya . . . oh, at least once in your life you should have an experience like that, brother,' proclaimed the good man with the full beard and even fuller stomach, which began to act up halfway through the journey, or so he said.

'Yes, go on.'

'When I lived in Libya . . . oh, what a time that was, my dear brother . . .'

'You mean Libya, as in Tripoli, delayed flights, sand-boxes and oil, *sidi hajji?*'

'Right, that's the one. I worked there from, oh let's say roughly from the oil crisis up until the earthquake in

Mexico. You could live the good life there, and by that I mean, brother, my good man, let me explain . . .'

'Wait! Let me finish your sentence for you, my dear *sidi hajji*: food and cholesterol galore, barbecued goat, curried rice and olala everywhere you looked?'

'By God, by Zeus, by whoever: you've certainly been well briefed! Anyway, I was working for an oil company . . . what a time that was, brother . . . and we used to get picked up every morning at our hotel and brought to the refinery by a surly, arrogant bus driver, a Libyan, and as God is my witness . . .'

The driver interrupted him: 'Let me guess, in between this curve and the next: he was an arrogant fathead, as arrogant as only fat conceited slobs like him can be. Am I right, my dear *sidi hajji?*'

'Hmm, not bad. In any case, pretty close to the truth . . . But what I wanted to say was, what arrogance! In fact I've noticed, my dear brother, that all those self-righteous hypocrites are good at tooting their own horns; you'd think they'd invented fire, the wheel and detergent ads single-handed! But anyway, what I wanted to say, brother, was . . .'

'Go ahead and say it *sidi hajji*,' prompted the driver, glancing sideways at Lamarat as he went into a curve that swerved towards Al Homey.

'. . . what I wanted to say was, wherever I've been, on pilgrimage, in Libya, in Egypt, on the Azhar campus . . . they all knew where I came from much sooner than I knew where they came from and they also knew exactly how to make me feel inferior. Do you agree with me or not, my dear brother?'

'Of course *sidi hajji*, who-is-my-elder-by-far, your words ring out with the crystal clarity of law, not to mention that in times like these a man of understanding is worth his weight in gold.'

'Hmm, hmm, that's true. But as you know gold is *haram*, which reminds me: you aren't insured, are you? Insurance is also forbidden, super *haram*, ugh, utter filth, you'll be careful, won't you?'

'Take it easy, *sidi hajji*, I promise I won't do anything to cause you a moment's grief. But do go on, *sidi hajji*, you make it all sound so uncommonly exciting.'

'Exactly, so if I may continue, because I haven't told you the worst part yet. You could hardly exchange three words with other Moroccans without having one of those fezzes make a remark about it being a third-rate language, and it was even worse if we spoke in our own Iwojen dialect, oh, oh, oh, then those guys would really have a field day. They made us feel like whipped dogs, do you know what I-who-am-your-elder-by-far mean or don't you, my dear brother?'

'You're so right.'

The driver curved again to the left and Al Homey – minaret, bricks, yellowed grass – lay at the bottom of the road, glistening like a filthy wad of cotton.

'My dear *hajji*, but what can I say about that time, or this time, or even this region . . ' (they're forever talking about Iwojen and how they'll be driving six white camels when they come, dum-di-dum) '. . . when fifty miles away there are people who think we're morons, in fact there are so many people who think we're morons that I've started to turn into one.'

'I'm glad to hear that you and I are of the same opinion. It's always a joy to travel with an understanding person like yourself, and just between you, me and the rocking chair, it looks like an anti-dialect epidemic has broken out; everywhere you go our people are at each other's throats, incredible, I sometimes wonder why in god's name I still wear a jellaba and carry a set of beads. Yes, people like me are also plagued by questions of faith, so now that we seem to be getting somewhere, I ask you: why have our people had so many prophets? Well, brother, if you have an answer, go ahead and spit it out. I mean, please forgive me for being so bold, but what I mean is: Moses, Jesus, the whole shebang, topped off like the jewel in the crown by our very own one-and-only Mohammed, praise be His name. If I may, godforgiveme, pose such an indelicate question, do you have any idea why there are so many?'

'I appreciate your honesty, *sidi hajji*, but I, a simple cabby, can't give you an answer to such a complex theological question. Forgive me, perhaps a discount on the fare will help make amends.'

'A discount – sure thing.' The *hajji*'s face cleared and immediately clouded again. 'And let me add that what we people need is a whip and a good thick plank. That way you can hit with both at the same time.'

In the short silence that followed, Lamarat got the distinct feeling that he'd wound up in a black comedy.

Suddenly, of his own accord, with no prompting, the *hajji* sat up in his seat and launched into an insane tirade. 'Shall I confess something to you, I mean really confess, no, not that I have millions of dirhams in the bank, everybody knows that, even you taxi drivers know that since I was clever enough to leak that secret through the walls of my house, but no, what I want to say is, sometimes I think to myself: my one wish, the one I want more than anything, is to have been born a Jew – preferably in, uh, what's it called, you know, New York, I mean just look at all the power they've got, okay, granted the whole country is bankrolled by America, may it rot in hell, and it's full of Jews, vipers, but they've got kibbutzim everywhere and the trees are loaded with oranges, grapes and Pepsi-Cola, or whatever that diabolical drink is called.'

The taxi driver's eyes opened wide, and he whispered

softly, 'I'll be damned, I've got a *korayshely*, a renegade, in my car.'

But the *hajji* wasn't through. 'You want more proof? Take a map, any map, most of them are made in Germany, but they can be trusted in spite of that, after all you know what the Germans did to the Jews (and to think they look down on *us*), but okay, look at the map and you'll notice one thing about the Middle-East: everything is dry, dry as a bone, not even a cactus would be able to grow in soil like that . . . except in one little corner: our Palestine. The Jews have turned that lousy bit of ground into super soil! Do you know what I'm saying, brother, of course you do – I'm not for the Jews, mind you, what Hitler did was right and we're waiting for a repeat, but sometimes in a flash of madness I think it would have been better if *we* had been sent to the gas chambers: by now we'd have our feet firmly on the ground, we'd be getting big bucks from America that we didn't have to exchange for fighter jets and Pepsi-Coca-Cola, and we wouldn't have to blow our own horn quite so loudly, if you know what I mean but of course you know what I mean . . .'

It was something of a miracle, the way the taxi driver could see what was happening behind him without looking in his rearview mirror, which he'd turned around out of a sense of propriety, and how he could follow the man's entire monologue without seeing his face. From then on until Lamarat got out in the parking lot in Al Homey, no one in the cab said a word. These people, he thought as he paid, are amazing. They wash their floors with Tide, eat prickly pears without having to resort to a laxative and go off from weddings without so much as a goodbye. And to think that I now belong to the same club: the Society Longing for a Custom-made Holocaust.

*

The sun was still high in the sky, The Observant One observed after he had arrived in Al Homey and left the taxi and its wayward passenger behind him. Lamarat walked around for a while, looking for the street that would take him to his cousin, the guy who might or might not be able to point him towards his uncle.

Unbelievable, the number of creatures you find crawling around these towns – cockroaches, donkeys, horses, and a wasp that kept buzzing around him, dogging his every footstep. If he'd had a rock, he would have thrown it at the wasp. But then again, he thought, killing a wasp might be just as hard as killing a cat. Cats are bigger but holier, wasps are smaller but deadlier. The balance: zero.

The person who had directed Lamarat towards his cousin was a guy called Ammunir, a young man in his late twenties, with blue eyes, red straw-like hair and a giant mole on the tip of his nose. He had a little shop across the street from their new house in Al Homey. Lamarat entered his bazaar just as Ammunir was busy winning from himself.

'I'm in the middle of a game, can't you see that? Leave me alone.' He threw high dice, he threw low dice, but mainly he threw lots of dice. So many dice that they – three brothers and three sisters, including one of marriageable age – had started referring to him as the Mad Gambler. Ammunir the Squanderer, the Screwball, the Wheeler Dealer, the Song and Dice Man.

'All those games are a waste of time, my son. They won't bring you money, a wife or respect,' said his mother in a woeful refrain. 'What do you hope to accomplish? What good are all those games? Why don't you swear off Parcheesi and try pushing those boxes of Tide instead?'

But he didn't stop, nor did detergent sales suffer; on the contrary, business was brisk. 'How many I sell? Well, let's see, in the morning lots, in the afternoon almost as many, and as evening falls I have a couple of late customers.'

To his mother he said, 'Woman, listen to me for once. I wish you'd quit nagging me, 'cause this is the only thing I can do and also happen to be good at!' And he threw another double six. Yippee, another red one home! Every day that he was open – and that was seven days a week, from eight o'clock in the morning to ten o'clock at night – he would play game after fast-paced game of Parcheesi with himself. The board was set up on the counter, and his fingers would zip from the coloured pawns to the dice as if his hand was being chased by a hornet. Eight pawns: one quartet of red and one quartet of yellow, and the game can begin. He refused, despite the many pleas of his brothers and sisters – 'Aw, please, just one game, say yes and I'll buy an extra box of that stupid Tide, hey c'mon man, don't be such a jerk!' – to play with anyone else. 'I'll be glad to tell you why,' he said, 'I'm way too good for you. I play better, much better than anyone else.' As a Parcheesi past master, he felt he couldn't lower himself to playing with others. And you had to admit, which his brothers and sisters did, that he was right. 'Parcheesi can't be taught – you either have it, or you don't,' Ammunir told the detergent-buyers and drop-ins, including Lamar-at, who asked him how he'd got so incredibly good that he was actually the only one capable of beating himself and what you had to do to become a crackerjack Parcheesi player. (According to local gossip, he continued to play in his sleep, in his dreams.) 'You can practise till you're blue in the face. Take me, for example, I was born in a hovel, surrounded by cactuses and five daily calls to prayer. I'm no different than you are. In fact, I'm less than you are – I walk with a limp.'

'Playing the handicapped card, are you?' the brothers and sisters would scoff, inadvertently adding fuel to the fire. 'A game of bravado-bluff-pokerface is more like it. A limp can't keep you from winning at Parcheesi. In fact, if it weren't for your handicap you wouldn't have learned how to play Parcheesi in the first place. After all, you didn't have to work in the fields, you didn't have to fetch water from the spring like other kids your age. Father always spared you the rod, the belt, his calloused hands, and all because you were crippled . . .'

Ammunir couldn't stand it when the attack got personal. 'Bullshit, baloney, bilge! Who's the one who has to sit lower than everyone else when we play? Me! Who's the one whose gammy leg keeps him from getting a good view of the table? Me! Look, let's say you and I are playing.' He shoved the board towards Lamarat. 'You can scooch around in your chair, sit up, look up, see which pawn is where, predict future moves from whatever position you want. But me? That left leg is stuck to my body like a block of wood – I can hardly see a thing. But it doesn't matter here. Every game I play against myself is a home game, so I can make it easy on myself and take any position I like, if you know what I mean. Listen carefully, because you missed your big chance when you were born . . .'

Lamarat couldn't really follow what Ammunir was saying. So he nodded his head the whole time, like a fast-ticking metronome: no-yes-no-yes.

'. . . look, when you were still sucking your mother's tits, I was already playing in the cafés along the highway, I know 'em all, know exactly how each cup of mint tea is made, what kind of hash they smoke, how many bags of sunflower seeds they sell a day and which café supports which football club. Personally I think Real Madrid stinks – those damn white T-shirts of theirs are impossible to keep clean. I played every day, with whoever came along, and I won from the lame, I won from the blind and I won from those who didn't see, but what you need to understand is that they didn't like me in those cafés, from the start, they don't like success, so they hated me, the people there, those kids I played against, those babies, because I didn't just win, I beat the socks off 'em. I was a feared and hated man because of the way I played, the way I threw the dice, moved the pawns and made the most of my luck – that's why I'm sitting here today. I was simply too good for those lowlifes and tea freaks. One day they said to me – I still remember every word, it was the Sunday after that Barcelona-Real Madrid match when the Catalans walked off with a victory – and even the café owners got into the act, no doubt because I always accepted whatever tea was offered but never, ever paid for a round myself: "Listen, Ammunir," they said, "we've had enough of your winner's mentality. Piss off!" I barely escaped their kicks and gobs of spit, and now I'm here. Say a prayer of thanks on my behalf. But the game must like me because it's brought me prosperity: Tide is selling like hot cakes with strawberry jam and I have enough time left over to play my own game . . .' (In the course of the last year or two he'd sold lots and lots of detergent to lots and lots of women, none of whom knew what he was up to with that crazy-coloured board and those accursed dice.) '. . . and every once in a while someone comes in here, he's heard of me, I was really good you know, an absolute genius, I mean it, my hand was golden . . .' He waved his fist in front of Lamarat's eyes as if he was about to tap a hammer on a sugar loaf wrapped in a dry tea towel. '. . . and the guy wants to challenge me to a game. But I say no. The only thing that motivates me is revenge, pure revenge . . .' (Those guys really cheese me off, but that's not surprising, seeing as how the game is called Parcheesi. Except that around here it's known as *parschee*.)

Lamarat was shocked at the accusations Ammunir

proceeded to hurl at the region in which they'd both been born. Surely there was no reason to be so harsh . . .

'After they kicked me out of the cafés, that piss-ant said, "Listen, fella, you can store this away for future reference. Nobody in Iwojen likes you. They all hate your guts." You know the guy I mean, Pimple Face.' (Ammunir had to laugh at his own meanness.) 'He's got a little bazaar in the city, and he sits there all day with his unsold jellabas and tapes, slurping tea and playing the hornpipe. The next time you see him remember what he said to me back then: "If you ever set foot in this café again, I swear I'll . . . Fuck off, you smell like pig piss!" Honest to god, that's what he said, even though he'd deny it, you know how he is, why are you looking at me like that. . . ?' (Who the hell does he mean, thought Lamarat, and shook his head.) '. . . there's no reason to shake your head, of course you know who I'm talking about, after all he's a relative of yours: he's your cousin. He and your uncle used to hang out together. He'd spend every day in your cousin's bazaar, that is if there wasn't anything he needed to do around here, if nobody needed cement or bricks or tiles, in other words, if his money wasn't needed to buy building materials. Your uncle's been good to me. He's different, he didn't have to win from me, but that cousin of yours . . . ! He gave me the shaft, but it boomeranged on him. Thanks to his envy and resentment, I'm now earning more in one week – especially since you people from the north are here – than he does in an entire year in that stupid bazaar of his . . .'

Ammunir ranted on for a while in the same vein, 'I hate him, I hate him, I hate him . . .' and momentarily lost interest in the game. In the meantime it occurred to Lamarat that a visit to his cousin might be a nice diversion. The days were long in that house and you had to do something (especially when your father and his father were constantly driving back and forth with pots and pans and the women spent all their time greeting one starved relative after another and stuffing them with almonds and pistachios). Ammunir, feverishly throwing the dice and scooting the pawns around the board, had sneered, 'Don't bother me when I'm playing, especially not when I'm winning from myself.' But he'd stood up and grudgingly pointed his finger towards the northern part of town and said, 'Keep going straight and you'll get there.' Then he'd shuffled back into his gaming den, with one hand clutching the two dice and the other clenched into a fist, mumbling to himself, 'I hate him, I hate him . . .'

Lamarat, pondering Ammunir's good fortune, walked past the cabinetmaker's – a one-man outfit where five boys under the age of fifteen were sanding, varnishing and carpentering – and then past the chicken slaughterhouse. Though it wasn't in any guidebook, the chicken slaughterhouse was the only noteworthy spot in Al Homey. In a room that measured no more than fifteen by fifteen feet, there were hundreds of chickens running around: all for sale. Next to the showroom there was a machine of some sort, manned by two boys who kept the cash flow in their righthand pockets. Let's suppose you're a customer. You go over to the two boys, point to an arbitrary member of the poultry family and ask for 'that one'. Sometimes the kid doesn't grab the chicken you want, but okay, you can't have everything. You decide not to mention this, and you ask him to kill the chicken. Which he does – it's part of the service. The job typically requires a prayer and a few quick slits with an orange-handled paring knife (made in Germany). Then comes the best part: while the chicken is still bleeding like a pig, the kid holds it up to the machine. This technological wonder consists of a barrel with rubber paddles attached to it. They switch it on, it starts whirling, they hold the chicken up to the rubber paddles and the feathers fly thick and fast into the washbasin. First they do the head, then the rear, and keep on going until there are no feathers left. The other kid grabs a white plastic bag, stuffs the chicken into it and takes your money. After that you can go home and, an hour later, serve up a delicious chicken dish. With potatoes, carrots and, of course, a sauce. (Don't forget to add a few strands of saffron).

Lamarat continued past this cultural highlight and soon reached the main street of Al Homey – the Singapore of North Africa, as Ammunir liked to refer to it – a broad street running all the way down to the beach pavilion and lined on both sides with a variety of shops selling plastic bags, leather jackets, flick-knives and other useful miscellany. The cousin's shop was on the corner, and the cousin, standing outside, had spotted him from afar. His face resembled a soft-boiled egg turned on its side, and in all probability consisted of sixty percent liquid acne.

'Hey there young man, Lamarat, the son of Minar, come over here, and don't tell me you don't know who I am,' the guy shouted. 'You're my cousin, we're second cousins, my mother is your mother's aunt . . .' And before Lamarat had time to say anything, he was yanked into the bazaar. 'Nice of you to come, we haven't been introduced before . . .' (he took another good look at Lamarat), '. . . but you haven't come here for a chat, someone sent you, it was that cripple, that Parcheesi fanatic, am I right or not?' He grinned and pulled up a pouffe. 'Is he still alive and has he lost against himself yet?'

There was a camel on the pouffe. A small, brown leather camel with a light bulb screwed into the hump on its back. Very popular with Spanish tourists.

'Sit down,' said his long-lost relative. At any rate

Lamarat thought of him as such, though the cousin was treating him like he'd been wandering in and out of the shop for years. Lamarat plucked the lamp from the pouffe, clamped it between his knees and sat down. The cousin stepped outside, 'I'll just go and get some tea, in honour of my new-found cousin,' and left Lamarat sitting with a lightbulb pressing into his crotch.

A few seconds later his cousin returned with an enamel tray, a big pot of tea and three glasses, just in case. 'Here you go,' he said and a stream of piss filled the glass. A treat to the eyes, watching a glass fill with a golden stream. Holding the pot in his right hand, the cousin raised it high in the air. Next he picked up a large – I repeat *large* – glass in his left hand and held it suspended above the tray. Then he gently tipped the pot and voilà: he peed into the glass, until a thick layer of foam indicated that it was time to stop. 'So, my dear cousin, here you go: a glass of our very own home-brewed beer.' What did he mean by that home-brewed business – did the mint leaves contain some kind of stimulant? Did you really flip out from all that guzzling and whoopee? The boy wasn't sure but accepted the glass anyway and tried to find a more comfortable position. While his cousin was gone he'd taken a quick look around. The shop, barely bigger than a fitting room, was filled to the brim with touristy knick-knacks and traditional Moroccan items. Up near the ceiling was a display of caftans and jellabas. Though jellabas have always been the Moroccan woman's everyday wear and party outfit, there are admittedly enough men these days who also like to parade around in these get-ups. There was also a black prayer robe with vertical stripes of exactly the prescribed width.

'Your uncle's bride is a real pearl! But there's no need to tell you that, you've known her for years.'

So the cousin had already seen his sister. Was nothing sacred anymore?

'The two of them went to Melilliar,' the cousin added.

'What did they do in Melilliar?' Lamarat asked.

'He sent your father and mother to the market-place and then took her to the park for a Spanish ice-cream cone.' The cousin laughed, exposing his tea-foam-coated teeth. A mint leaf was stuck to his front tooth.

'In the park, near the Place de España, she put her arm through his. Up till then he'd been keeping his arms stiffly at his side. He was surprised. But she said, "Arm in arm. That's how we walk in Europe".' The cousin laughed even harder. 'Because of that one gesture uncle dear had three sleepless nights. No other woman has ever thrown him for such a loop . . '

'So he's had other women?'

Just then something caught the cousin's eye, and he dashed outside, calling loudly, 'Chatischa, Chatischa!' A diminutive young lady walked over to him. She was wearing sunglasses and her hair was pulled back in a French knot, from which a few wisps had tantalizingly escaped. His cousin flapped his hands, turned his head this way and that, going overboard on the gestures and smiling at the slightest sign of encouragement. He kept touching her, as if he wanted to let her know his attention was genuine. Her skin-tight dress came to just above her knees, and her tiny feet were shod in sandals. Under her arm she was clutching a leather bag with gold-plated letters dangling from the zip. A girlfriend perhaps, family? Hardly, Lamarat thought, she was far too voluptuous. Maybe a casual acquaintance, a former classmate, a customer? She nodded a couple of times, he touched her cheek again, she allowed his every intimacy, and then they parted. His brand-new cousin came back into the shop and sat down on the pouffe across from Lamarat.

His pimples had turned bright red, and they looked like they were going to burst into flame any moment.

'She's hot to trot.' Lamarat didn't say anything – next it'd be his sister. 'I'm going to Melilliar with her tomorrow. We'll see what happens.' Lamarat stared at his cousin in total incomprehension until the man finally broke into loud guffaws. He stood up and reached behind the counter for a pen, which he toyed with while he softly drawled, 'Well, your uncle's girl – she was, and hopefully still is, a real pearl . . .'

(A pearl who would soon have to prove her worth in bed. The parents of the bride agreed on this point: their daughter was pure as the driven snow, both inside and out. She would have no trouble proving that she had been hoarding her virginity her entire life.)

One of the burning questions on the tip of Lamarat's tongue was: what happens on the big night?

'Tell me something, cousin. Soon the bride and bridegroom will be going to bed together. How does this wedding-night business work?'

The cousin sat down on a pouffe, a black one that he would sell to Spanish tourists at twice the going rate. He told the boy that the wedding would go pretty much as he pictured it, with lots of songs and recitations that he didn't know so wouldn't be able to sing along with. 'The celebration goes on until nightfall, the bridal chamber is furnished, though that won't happen in this case since he's leaving anyway, and then most of the people go home.'

'Not without having first polished off everything in sight, of course.'

'Of course. All those farmers ever do is eat and plough.'

'And then the bridegroom is expected to do his part. To deflower the bride.'

'Right.'

'And then?'

'Then, once that's over, he comes outside and sets off a skyrocket – of course he only does that if everything's gone alright.'

'Of course, if everything's gone alright . . . And if it hasn't gone alright?'

'You mean if there isn't a bloodstain? Well, in that case it's sorry, too bad, next girl better, ship this one back to her parents, *adiós* and goodbye.'

'Would he really do that . . . ? If, you know . . .'

'What? Your uncle and your sister? No way! Nah, that guy's so anxious to get out of here he'd marry a turtle if he thought that'd get him to Deutschland or wherever it is you live. Besides, if there isn't a bloodstain', said the cousin, 'he'll prick his fingers with a pin and let the blood drip on to the sheet, because of course we don't want to, you know, make a big thing out of it . . .'

All this had taken place a few days before Lamarat came back to Al Homey. This time he slunk into the shop and found his cousin holding two glasses of tea in his hands.

'Hi there, cousin, is that you again? Who? Oh, you're looking for your uncle. No, I couldn't tell you exactly where he is, but I have a sneaking suspicion that he . . . that he's . . . that he might have taken himself off to Melilliar, to a bar . . . The address? After you get to Melilliar, walk down this street and then that street, and, oh yeah, when you see him tell him I said hello . . .'

God's grotto

It's time – now that the uncle has been found and is snoring away in the back seat, Lamarat is wondering if and when he'll wake up, and the taxi is trundling up and down the hills – to toy with the truth, a truth that's already taken quite a beating from me, because how can you expect anyone to believe that a lousy little nail could put an end to a human life, that a farm kid missed his calling as a Parcheesi hustler and – the most unlikely of all, even for me – that a house could moulder and decay, without the least bit of natural or human intervention, until it was nothing more than dust and wind.

One notch up the unlikeliness scale is the story the main character never let himself be told. (Nobody had ever mentioned it to him and probably nobody ever would, but whenever Lamarat ran into anyone who had known him since he was a baby – and that included many people in various parts of the globe, even as far away as Patagonia – a light would click on in their heads and they would remember his birth. In one gigasecond the event would be shown in instant replay. Still, they were careful not to blurt it out to him – it isn't right to gossip about others.)

You see, Lamarat was born in a story that has a high magic-trick quotient: the story – here it comes – of the covenant between the grandmother and Sidi Rabbi.

It may be so, or it may not be so, in any case it's so-so, but the people of Iwojen don't like to forget things, which means that this truthful lie, this self-explanatory figment of a vivid imagination, must contain a smidgen, a teeny-weeny kernel of truth. But what difference does it make? I'm just going to tell it and see where it takes us.

The story of Grandma and God, of the *mtsimeni* maker and the Prime Mover (as Mosa the Samaritan was fond of calling his member), was told up and down every hill and dale in Iwojen. It was on every lip just after Lamarat had been born. However, everything erodes in time. It eventually blows over, flies off and all that's left is an, 'Oh, yeah, back then, those were the days.' Right after it happened it was the subject of serious reflection by the girls at the spring, the boys on the way to the spring, and the men in the maize fields around the spring. 'Did she really receive a message from God, and if so, why in God's name did He send it to her, the *mtsimeni* dame?' Before long the event had been reduced to something you wondered about or laughed at. After all, the people of Iwojen might not forget things, but their attitude towards them did change. So by the time houses with electricity and running water were being built in Al Homey, the story had become, to anyone familiar with Iwojen, a miracle that rarely came up for discussion anymore. It had been demoted to a mini-miracle, replaced by newer and bigger miracles such as Amstel beer, air-soled trainers and satellite dishes that bring tits and cunts into the living room, flagrantly, in full living colour.

Yet if there's anything nicer than a miracle, it's gossip. And, according to Bucket of Bolts Chalid, the very nicest of all is a secret packaged as gossip. His knowledge of the conversation between Grandma and God dated back to the days when he used to roam over the rocks and ruts in

Iwojen and hear the laughter of the men waiting by the spring for the girls, who had such a delightful way of clacking their tongues. 'What's so funny?' Chalid asked. 'Just an old story, from years ago, maybe you still remember it, the one about the old lady and her daughter-in-law.'

'Tell me, tell me,' he said. And so they told him, repeating the story for his benefit, because the girls hadn't come yet and because it was interesting and at the same time . . . strange.

The day that Lamarat the Lucky was born, the men were off ploughing and the children of Iwojen were down by the frog ponds making dolls out of clay. In other words it was a day in which the maximum had to be achieved with the minimum of means. The first contractions were felt by the boy's future mother at about 8.00 a.m. She was lying in bed by herself that morning, because the future father was off doing his daily stint at a shipyard that, unbeknownst to him, was about to go belly up. She suddenly realized that she'd never had to work so hard in her life, and she immediately regretted the plan she'd hatched one diabolical night. But it was too late – she had no choice but to push. The future grandmother, awakened in the early morning by the screams, donned a special scarf – her childbirthing scarf – and rushed to the expectant mother's aid. She held her hand, unable to do much more than pray. No doctor was available to lend the proceedings an aura of medical expertise because back in those days nobody had a phone, and besides there was a long tradition of midwifery – the women with the most experience acted as midwife. This time, in the absence of anyone more qualified, the job fell to the grandmother.

The mother-to-be yelled her head off. It wasn't until late in the afternoon that the child emerged from God's grotto. You see, God is loathe to entrust his children to inhuman nature; a woman has to work hard, fight for her child, show that she deserved the tiny babe suckling at her breast.

This and much more the grandmother knew, since she had dreamed about it, had spoken about it to God.

It came to the driver's ears from the most reliable of sources – the gossips in and around Iwojen – that the strange, prophetic dream had occurred a few weeks before the baby's birth, soon after Ramadan. (Or was it the Day of Sacrifice? Calendars were scarce in Iwojen.) The grandmother had supposedly told her dream to the women at the spring. She claimed that a voice had spoken to her, saying that nobody knew when the child would be born, and furthermore that the father would not be there to see the child come into the world in a gush of blood, pee and poop. God then apparently exited with the words: *the mouth of a woman can either make or break a person*. For the benefit of the astonished bystanders, the *mtsimeni* queen repeated it three times. It had been ages since the women at the spring had heard such a magical incantation. Even the older women, older than the grandmother who foretold the future with stones, lowered their arms and recited a few prayers to protect God's words from any evil spirits that might be lurking around the spring.

The grandmother had been both surprised and puzzled by the message. After all, you always knew the due date, and the father had saved up enough money and vacation days so he could be on hand to help celebrate the birth of his child. The grandmother was advised to be on the alert and not to let the expectant mother out of her sight for a minute; it was also a good idea to hide several bags of salt in the house before the big event to ward off any *jnoon* who might be floating around.

The dream had almost been forgotten when the father – who had been welcomed back to the village a month before the baby was due with the minimum of fanfare ('Why bother, it's not the Prophet') – suddenly left again. He disappeared in the night, apologizing for the rush, but duty called. Work, work, work, to pay for houses in many cities. His mother hadn't understood why her son had abruptly packed his bags and succumbed to the tyranny of the time clock. 'Your child is going to be born, dammit,' were her exact words, but he seemed all too relieved that he wasn't going to be around for the arrival of his firstborn. So one of the prophecies had come true. Now that grandma's soothsaying credentials had been firmly established, the handful of women at the spring who had initially dismissed her vision with a time-honoured gesture of 'hooey' now had to backtrack and ask if she'd also dreamed about *their* children.

That left another prophecy and one cryptic statement, but as it turns out both of them came true the day of the birth. What happened, or so the driver gathered from a variety of clacking tongues, was that the grandmother had started to make *mtsimeni* that morning. She had kneaded a mixture of flour, milk and dry yeast in a wooden bowl until it was the size of a large football, divided the football into tennis balls and then flattened the tennis balls into squares, exactly ten squares. And ten is not a magic number in these parts. She plopped the squares on to a blackened griddle, sprinkled a few drops of olive oil on them and let them sizzle and sigh, square after square. Then she took a rusty pair of scissors out of her pocket – 'and this is crucial,' the old men of the region told each other as the driver, then a young man, listened to them talk, 'because she went outside and used those rusty scissors to cut off a few mint leaves.'

'Exactly,' the old men echoed one another, down by the

village crossroads where they would meet after they finished ploughing, threshing and picking grapes. 'And just as she was snipping off a leaf, she heard the mother-to-be bringing her child-to-be into the world.' A miracle, a miracle, and the biggest miracle of all was that the terrified grandmother rushed to the room, the same room in which the bride and bridegroom-to-be are supposed to celebrate their union tonight – an intriguing detail, the taxi driver thought – and found her daughter-in-law in the middle of the most excruciating contractions. The grandmother helped bring the child into the world as best she could, while the men threshed the grain and the village children played in the fertile clay. After the boy had made his appearance with the requisite number of fingers and toes and was slithering around in the pee and the poop, the grandmother remembered that the umbilical cord, the contact between heaven and earth, had to be severed, or else the child would never belong to its mother. 'Only then did she realize that the scissors, those rusty old scissors that had helped bring dozens of children into the world, had been left out in the yard when she was cutting the mint leaves.'

And then the biggest miracle of all occurred, the part the old men like to ponder best: she couldn't find the scissors. They were gone, swallowed up by the earth. That was impressive, but also scary, the taxi driver thought; he had shivered the first time he had heard this story, and now, as a grown man, he shivered again. He looked over at the boy, who was talking about Al Homey and about how little sun the house got.

. . . at that moment the second prophecy came true: the grandmother had no choice (or couldn't come up with an alternative fast enough) but to *bite* the umbilical cord in two. She bit down hard, actually crushing it more than biting it, and all the while the ten square *mtsimeni* were burning to a crisp. It was only when she felt the bloody umbilical cord in her mouth that she remembered the words of God. But by that time the baby was resting peacefully in the arms of the earth's newest mother.

The boy in the story, the one sitting beside the driver, he whose umbilical cord had been bitten in two, had never heard the story. Nobody in Al Homey had ever told it to him – certainly not Ammunir, who only listened to the stories whispered to him by the game. No one, not now or ten years ago when he was last here, had ever breathed a word to him of what had happened to the grandmother, the mother and the boy.

Recipes for love

The Do-As-I-Do-Course, Part I, Lesson 1, *Cooking for Two*: take a village located on good, salty seawater and pour in half a cup each of a man and a woman. Add a layer of holy matrimony of the first pressing, letting the oil simmer slowly on the first day until by the second or third day it will be warm enough to add the guests (having first discarded their tender green shoots), plus their mouths, drums and wives (*ooee ooee ooee* – thattaway, Mother). Stir this mixture, preferably with a wooden spoon that has been used for other weddings since this will ensure such nebulous things as happiness and good fortune, or so they say, though you won't find it in any cookbook. Believe me.

In the meantime, place several rings of bearded men in a shallow frying pan and sauté them over a low heat until they're golden brown. Let them simmer for a while, keeping a close watch on them, then add a handful of bank notes to help thicken the sauce. Check the main ingredients – the man and the woman – from time to time since they will need to be removed after a few hours, rinsed with cold spring water, wrapped in two white towels, dried thoroughly and then baked – needless to say *separately* – in a 350° or 400° preheated oven until the man is well done and the woman medium rare. When they're an even brown, test them by pricking them with a fork to see if they bleed. (Don't worry if the man is underdone. They always seem to come out half-baked.) Put the meat, the fried rings and the sea consommé in a cool place and wait one year, two years, fifty years – it depends on what happens. Observe closely, don't touch, let matters take their course.

Feel free to add other ingredients to this recipe, such as maize, rice, coriander, peppers, greenhouse tomatoes, pickles and maternity leave (preferably topped with whipped cream). Bon appétit!

Chalid began to get hungry as they approached Touarirt. He tried to still his longing for meat and butter by fantasizing about the dishes being served the wedding guests; he thought of the cooking pots, the stomachs, the lambs being chopped up one by one. He thought of the many sheep that had been slaughtered on the eve and morning of the first day of the wedding, how they'd been hung up alive in the sheep shed and how a local expert, a man with hardly a tooth in his mouth, had slit their throats. He thought of the warm blood that had streamed down and the steamy heat that had risen up from the sheep. Next, the man had skinned the animal with a paring knife, chopped off its head and handed over the insides – liver, heart, lungs, stomach, intestines, kidneys, spleen and testicles – to a woman of equal expertise who had flung them into a bucket. A little water had been added and a band of young women, some with babies on their backs, had taken charge of the pile. One washed the heart and cleared the aorta of coagulated blood, another scraped the brown gunk off the tripe, the third cut the lungs into pieces and tossed them into a waiting pan, the fourth peeled the skin off the testicles and sliced them in half, and someone else removed the fat from the kidneys, which was saved since it would later be added to the meat to enhance the flavour of the sauce. Then the spleen, the liver, the tripe and the intestines, the green goo having been squeezed out of them, were thrown in a pan and put on the fire.

A few hours later the first offer of the wedding was ready to be served: a strong, occasionally overpowering dish of offal. By that time the local expert had removed the sheepskin and the mother of the house had smeared salt on the inside and put it on the roof to dry. Then the carcass, devoid of any extraneous bits, was hacked into pieces with a rusty axe (how many weddings do you suppose that axe had presided over?). The shoulders, legs and hindquarters were cut into smaller chunks and dumped into a huge, three-foot wide cauldron bubbling away over the fire. Add tomatoes, olives and green beans and let it simmer.

Just as a firefly was flying through the moon for the third time, Lamarat got out of the cab and then pulled his uncle out. Mosa leaned against him with his full weight and, still snorting and mumbling, took a bank note out of his pocket, then another one, and another one, thanks Chalid, see ya' around. The taxi roared off and raced towards harbour and home.

'Ha!' said Lamarat when he and Mosa were left standing beside the path that wound its way to Touarirt over Sugar Mountain. 'We're on our own now, it's just you and me – and all the people waiting for you. Mosa, gosa, losa, King of the Cold Feet, it's time we got going, time we went to *your* wedding by the sea!' And Lamarat tightened his grip on his uncle and began to carry him down the mountain.

On Lamarat's first visit to Iwojen, Mosa had taken him to the sea almost every day. Every morning after breakfast he'd rustle up a pair of underpants and a worn towel and say, 'Okay, I'll do it, but only because I know how much it means to you.' First he'd go out back to take a leak, and while the golden shower was splashing on to the field behind the house, he'd tell Lamarat how the sea looked that day. He'd light up another cigarette – during holidays he'd switch to Marlboro 'since Casa Sport tastes like a cross between dung and dried thistles,' and focus his glassy gaze on the sea while the clay soil would cling to the rubber sandals he'd bought in Melilliar.

The sea had a different face every day. Sometimes it was taut like a sheet of aluminium foil. Beautiful. If you scanned the horizon you could see a few wrinkles forming around the edge but the overall picture would remain the same. As they went down the hill – a mile or so – over that last steep, rocky stretch, Lamarat would think, today the sea's gonna stay like this and I'll be able to walk across it, like Jesus. But once he got down there, the sea would have changed, would have pulled a fast one on him, would be as wet as ever. So that's what the uncle meant by 'calm', as in, 'it's calmed down, it's no longer wild.'

Sometimes, when the sky draped itself over Sugar Mountain like a grey veil (though it would lift a few hours later), the uncle would say that the sea was choppy – and it would be. The water was troubled. Everywhere you looked there'd be teardrops and flecks of foam.

One time he went down to the beach anyway, curious to know what it was like. The sea had been dirty – he had swum around twigs, bits of Styrofoam and seaweed. But never mind, he'd had the entire sea to himself.

His uncle once told him the story of *his* uncle, Grandpa's brother, who was a confirmed beachcomber. He would scour the beaches in hopes of great treasure. Then one day he came across a plastic tub with an ice-cream logo. He lugged it up the mountain and threw it on top of the other junk he'd collected. When they finally got around to opening it up, they discovered it was full of shit.

The uncle hardly ever swam though his thin, wiry body seemed to be made for the water. He spent most of his time sitting in the shade, listening to tapes and treating himself to a Marlboro. Lamarat would hurly-burly his way down the steep hill behind Mosa's tall, thin frame. While he dived, floated and cavorted with the boys from the village, his uncle would sit under a bare rock and fiddle with the radio. He liked Berber music; Lamarat was unable to appreciate the women's high tones or the men's low innuendoes though he was getting better at it. After he'd swum to his heart's content, they'd go back up the mountain. And believe me, it was quite a hike.

He and his uncle and the boys from the village used to sit in a small bay, where the sea washed up in a lacy froth. There was a big rock jutting out of the sea, and some of the boys used to climb up on it and then dive into the water. Mosa would scoff. He told Lamarat that his big brother, Lamarat's father, was the first kid that had ever dared to dive off the rock. Lamarat had never known that his father had been such a hero.

The taxi driver, who hadn't been to the sea in years (work, work, work and more work – you know how that goes) had arrived home, and while Lamarat was feeling his way, with his uncle on his back, over a rocky path that was a lot bumpier in the dark than in the daytime, Chalid was fixing himself a nightcap, like one of those nine-to-five types in films: whisky and water. This was a highly unusual combination: whisky (nobody else in Iwojen drank whisky) mixed with tap water (nobody else had running water). And as he drank, he thought back to the drive. A real worrywart, that Lamarat. Wanting to tell so much and yet needing to bring back his uncle who kept repeating the same thing over and over, 'Hey, Ilovemybeer, hey, do you hear me, Ilovemybeer, Ilovemybeer.' And again, 'Ilovemybeer.'

With a whisky glass in his hand, Bucket of Bolts Chalid walked out of his house, a house with tiles that didn't fall off, a house with a view of Sugar Mountain and the highway, but not of the sea.

Mosa was tired but happy, just the way you're supposed to be. Avoiding Lamarat's eyes, he told the taxi driver who was bringing him back why he'd run away. 'I was supposed to be getting married tonight, you know, but women are, you know, difficult, do you get my drift or don't you, and by the way have you heard the story of the man who went to Patagonia to get away from everyone? That's what I should do – get the hell out of here.'

While Bucket of Bolts Chalid is gulping his whisky and looking out over his property, two feet – first one and then the other – are stumbling over the rocks, and the brain attached to those feet is beginning to wonder: how am I going to break the news to my sister? And while all of this and much more is happening in Iwojen – that anthill by the sea that's losing more and more of its population – a twenty-year-old girl decides to quietly leave her house, her father, her mother, her grandmother, her grandfather and all the other unwanted guests so she can find a spot in which to calm her nerves. No no, not the cactus field, that's out, it belongs to, you know, those two, the Beauty and the Dumbo, but maybe you can find somewhere else to sit.

And what better place to sit than in a cemetery? 'Hello, ancestors. Did your weddings always go like clockwork too? Also without a single hitch?' The girl touches the

164

gravestones, which are arranged in a circle, one by one. I'm going to sit here and never get up again, sister dear thinks. I'm going to sit here and only get up to kill him, sister promises herself. You can sprinkle me with as many spices as you want, with as much basil as you want, with all the hot pepper you desire, but you're not going to get away with this, Mosa. Sister is tired of waiting.

What Lamarat liked about Mosa was that he'd always taken the time to do things with him. Ten years ago, when Lamarat had served a happy six-week sentence in Touarirt, Mosa sometimes – well actually every day – got out a board with eighty squares, two times four pawns (blue and black) and two gnawed dice. 'It's time for a little *parschee*, do you comprendo, mio kiddo? It's not hard: toss the dice, throw a six, and move your men,' and I'll be darned if Lamarat didn't win and win, until Mosa finally called it quits. 'Too bad,' he said, as he put the board, the dice and the pawns in a cardboard box and shoved it under a stack of scratchy blankets, 'too bad you didn't stay here. You could have become the all-Iwojen world champion, you could have beat the crippled, the blind and the deaf, which is all we've got around here.'

'You know what, my dear nephew?' To Lamarat's surprise Mosa suddenly woke with a start. 'What can I say? You probably think I'm a drunk, a skunk . . .'
    Lamarat craned his neck to look at him, but Mosa was making no move to get down.
    '. . . a sleazeball, but of course I love your sister, I'd do anything for her, but sorry, don't forget I'm drunk, she doesn't mean a thing to me. Sure, she's a nice girl, respectable and all, but there's more . . .'
    At the end of the path, behind the fields between 'The Wind of San Antonio' and 'Our House', he could just

make out 'The Wolf's Den'. Over there, thought Lamarat, there's a house full of people – his father, his brother, his entire family – who could wring Mosa's neck, and he tells me Rebekka means nothing to him and that there's 'more'.

'Do you know what I'm saying, my dear nephew, or . . . '

'No, I don't know,' Lamarat finished his sentence for him and schlepped him further.

'IlovemybeerIlovemybeer,' Mosa mumbled in his ear. 'There's more, plenty more, so many more women that I've lost count. I can't seem to tear myself away from 'em. One's good at this, the other's good at that, I can't see the harm in plucking the fruits of both, if you know what I mean.' At the thought of Chatischa, his voice seemed to sparkle. 'Such a variety of talents, and soon my little paradise will be gone, I will have exchanged it for a banshee who beats me on the back!'

'Is that the reason, uncle dear?' said Lamarat. 'Just because you won't be able to dip your wick in all those different honey pots? Is *that* the reason you don't feel up to getting married, that you can't stomach the thought of the wedding – is that the only reason?'

'No, no, ha ha, no, no, of course not!' Mosa laughed shamelessly. 'Of course it isn't just *that*! But don't you understand that – that – that I'm a man, damn it! I'm a *man* and a man has to hide behind something, has to shield himself somehow so he can do whatever he wants to . . . By the way, my dear nephew, have you ever, ha ha, drunk Ricard – you know, the stuff that's as colourless as water when it's in the bottle, but turns into a white ghost the minute it hits the glass? Well, nephew, I'm kinda like that, like Ricard: invisible to the outside world; oh, I wait patiently enough, but I hide my true colours, my ghostly self, my real self. And nobody, but nobody knows what

I'm really like, not even a taxi driver, ha ha, hee hee, hic hic, I could die laughing . . !'

He isn't making a lick of sense, thought Lamarat. 'Cut the crap,' he said. 'It's all double Dutch to me.'

'Whoa, nephew baby, no need to be so flip, after all you know what Ricard is like: one glass is nice, two are even better, drink too many and you're off it forever.' And he boomed into the hot steamy night:

Bonitawiththebigtits
Olgalinawiththebigass
BahinaIwannakissyou
DarifaIgottago
Andthebestofall
Chatischascatterbrainslayerofmyvoice!

'Oh, girls, why do your names all end in that funny A and why do I owe you so much money and why, last unanswered question, am I unable or don't have the guts to tear myself away from you?' Turning to Lamarat he said, 'My dear nephew, say this to your sister or my brother: can't they put their big mouths to work and help free me from the white ghosts of my past? If they can do that with a wave of their abracadabra hands, you have my permission to ask them.'

Lamarat didn't have a clue what Mosa was talking about. The words wouldn't stay put but kept fluttering around his head, looking for a net. If he could capture the sounds the uncle was making, he could examine them and maybe even comprehend them. Lamarat didn't answer, but kept making his way down Sugar Mountain. He wanted the unspeakable to remain unspoken, he didn't want to believe that his drunken uncle couldn't see the difference between Chatischa and his sister, that he was scared of finding out, despite the upward mobility he envisioned for himself – a residence permit and tinned corn (made in Denmark) – that he would still be the same: a man deprived of Chatischas, Dinas, and Olginas, a guy who wanted to live forever in a Lolita world. But he let the unspeakable remain unspoken and groped with two hands for two other hands that were clutching a past that was better and infinitely more fun.

Lamarat, still carrying his uncle (who once again starts chanting 'Ilovemybeer'), staggers down the footpath and suddenly remembers all the sixes he used to throw. Sometimes, much to Mosa's surprise, he'd throw eight in a row. The house, glowing in the light of a lantern, is getting closer, the footpath over Sugar Mountain is gradually levelling off, and Bucket of Bolts Chalid has decided to go to bed, confident that the epilogue will be told in his dream.

(Instead Chalid dreams of sheep heads, detergent, a thousand times one thousand lottery tickets sold by a lame blind man in Melilliar and a voice that says, 'Don't believe in dreams, trust to luck.')

Exit taxi driver, which leaves us with Lamarat, who hears terrifying rustles and squeaks from behind the bushes, a voice reciting 'eeny, meeny, miney, moe,' and, last but not least, Miss Mouse herself, lying in state on a tombstone. Sister, promising herself that she'll put a curse on Mosa and call down spirits to destroy him, starts muttering in Iwojen dialect, 'May he be eaten alive by the Devil, may Shitan make him sick in the head, may he be swallowed up by fire, may I die if he ever has another woman.' The voice can be heard: loud and clear.

Unbelievable. Lamarat leaps off the footpath and beats his way through the bushes, because if his ears are not deceiving him (and they're not), someone is cursing like mad. It's definitely a woman's voice, and who else could it be . . . 'Rebekka, stop raving, will ya! What the heck are you doing here anyway!?'

After Rebekka had clapped her hand over Lamarat's mouth and boxed his ears, she asked him if he'd found her intended, her future husband-till-death-do-us-in. 'He's over there,' he pointed towards the path, 'he's passed out.' Rebekka beat her way through the bushes and indeed, there he was, stretched out on the path. She examined his snoring mouth, circled around him seven times, bent down and pinched his nose. 'Hel-lo, anybody home? Ohhh, you don't want to wake up? Well, if you need your little nappie-poo so much you can just stay where you are, you crud.' She stood up, looked at Lamarat, threw up her hands and said, 'Ratface, Ratface, wherefore art thou Ratface? Deny thy father and refuse that bloody awful name!'

'And as for this guy,' said Rebekka, 'we're going to give him a cold shower. Pick him up him by his ass, the no-good bum.' Then she bent over, grabbed him under the arms, murmured in his ear, 'I love you, breaker of my heart and total jerk,' and yanked him to his feet. 'Sweet, sexy Mosa, I love you so much if only you knew how much I wanted us to have so many good times why I'd be willing to circumcise you all over again if it means I could have you all to myself.' Rebekka turned to Lamarat. 'If you only knew, sweet, innocent Ratty, how I watched you run up and down the street when I was a little girl and dreamed of a wedding by the sea: a roaring fire, a huge bowl of punch, guitar music everywhere and a husband who'd wait on me hand and foot. "Here, darling, a bit more sand over your toes, there, precious, another pillow for your head, how about some juice from this pine-apple . . ." Humph, in this godforsaken village you can't get lighters, punch or glasses, but there's plenty of sea, more than enough sea . . . Come on,' sister shouted, 'we're going to the sea. And remember: we're taking that scuzzbag with us.'

Lamarat, lugging his uncle on his back as if he were a donkey with a load of grapes, was getting more and more confused (what'll the guests think what'll Father say what'll Mother do?) and he thought something that I too am thinking – for the umpty-umpth time: *you ought to picture the whole thing as if it's a puppet show.*

Hmm, that puppet theatre. How did that go, when all has been said and done? A stage filled with puppets. It's beginning to come back to me now: a stage full of girl puppets and boy puppets, each with its own colour . . . clothing . . . rigid symbolism . . . funny, how that came to mind . . . out of nowhere, hey presto, and there it was on the page. It served absolutely no purpose, and yet the doubts are beginning to creep in. I may have made a *terrible* mistake. So let's scratch the puppet metaphor, give it the old heave-ho, and concentrate instead on the night, the cemetery and the most beautiful puppet of all: the sister Rebekka, the puppet who brought Mosa back where he belonged: the sea he had never dared to swim in.

As they made their way down, over narrow footpaths, rocks and squished frogs, with Lamarat supporting Mosa on the right and Rebecca on the left, she said, 'When we were in the park, that sweetie-pie said to me, "There's only one woman I can really love, and that's you. I've been dreaming of you since the day I was born." Then Father came to me there in the bridal chamber and said, "Take it easy, he's gone out for a while, he's gone to the bathroom, he's freshening up, nothing's the matter, you know how men are, always busy, busy, busy, but just stay calm, try not to wipe the kohl from your eyes, just be your beautiful self and pretend that nothing's the matter," and off he went, to be with the guys and men, and who should come in a second later but Mother. She starts telling me, man I didn't know she needed to get so much off her chest, that "things are different nowadays, when I married your father I also found myself sitting in this room, frozen with fear, more scared than when your brother was born, 'cause thank goodness your grandmother was there to give me a helping hand, but that night, god was he ever bad, I've never dared tell this to anyone but we might as well be honest: *I* had to do all the work and I said to him, Didn't you learn anything from the movies in Melilliar, did you think they were doing a jig or what? But in the end everything was okay, there was a huge bloodstain on the sheet, try to beat that, my daughter, and he got better at it, your father was one of those goody-goody types, the kind of guy who wouldn't dare go to those women in the city to learn how to do it. . ." but why are you looking at me so strangely, my brother, my big goofy brother, it's true: she blurted it out like she'd been saving it up for tonight when I'd be transformed into a woman of the world and then she couldn't stop herself you know how it is with naughty girls once they get going they go all the way to heaven and hell and back again but then she said that she liked me more than you so now you've heard it from someone else my brother plus she said that I stayed in her stomach the whole nine months which pleased her no end if that makes any sense but what's even funnier is that she thinks my being born in a hospital was really neat and what she remembers most of all were the bananas and the grapes that Daddy brought her and the nurses who did everything for her even wiping her ass because she supposedly had back pains um it felt so good she said to lie there in

171

the hospital and do absolutely nothing that she turned into a sloth overnight if that makes any sense and she apologized for all those mornings when she didn't get out of bed but she likes to sleep late which isn't her fault because her mother spoiled her rotten and for not being a very good cook though I can't say I ever noticed but she seemed to mind even though it wasn't her fault that they had so much money when she was a child that she didn't have to lift a finger and could live it up but she's embarrassed to think of all the time she wasted and then she started in again on my problems and said just lie there child and when he climbs on top of you spread your legs and let him do all the work don't butt in don't say a word just pretend you're a raw meatball that he can prick however he wants but what if he asks me to do something then don't do more than he asks you to I mean if he wants you to assume another position go ahead but don't overdo it and oh yeah don't ever laugh at him or let him see how disappointed you are though in this case it probably won't be all that bad since I gather he's already figured out the basics or at any rate judging from the stories I've heard from Mother and the other women he's had a whole slew of whores and really screwed up our house which is a real disgrace but what can you do he's a man and those whores are everywhere I mean everywhere snorting that white powder or whatever that stuff is called just like the men they're hustling junkies every last one of them it's incredible and I'll tell you honestly brother when I heard her say that I began to get a bit panicky at the thought of tonight because let's suppose he does do stuff like that and those girlfriends of his too but on the other hand how could he afford it oh Lamarat my dear brother I'm so scared and it feels like I'm suspended in mid-air and could explode any minute though it doesn't give me a thrill which reminds me do you remember how my girlfriends used to dare me to do crazy things and how we'd swipe marbles from the toy shops you know there'd be these bins full of smurfs and pirates next to the cash register and they'd watch us like hawks but if they turned away for a second we'd stuff a couple of marbles in our mouths and then a couple more until your whole mouth was full boy you should have seen me trying to say goodbye as I went through the door and then I'd race around the corner and spit them out 'cause I was so scared I'd swallow the marbles that I couldn't hold them in very long hardly a minute but that black girl you know the one I mean the one who always had two fingers stuck in her mouth maybe that's why it was so big anyway one time she managed to cram in thirty marbles now that's really a mouthful and nobody noticed a thing until she ran outside or rather she was trying to run but they were working on the street and she fell bang right on her face and had to be taken to the hospital by the people from the toy shop god what a funny way to catch a thief because the marbles had got lodged in her lungs and oesophagus but how did I ever get off on that story I guess I'm just scared of him of tonight of catching some awful disease but I think I told you that story a long time ago anyway stealing gives you another kind of thrill and right now I feel scared because what if he doesn't come what if he doesn't want me I mean I've gone horseback riding which can tear you down there and swimming isn't good either but what does it matter since there are enough tricks and Mother said she'd still love me if there wasn't any blood but that I'd have to play my cards right and move my hips to his rhythm a bit and cry a lot and then he'd dribble some of his own blood on to the sheet and in any case I have a safety pin and scissors in my pocket god you really seem to be getting an earful but hopefully you won't be shocked 'cause after all we girls are so much smarter than you guys all you ever want is to win win win you might as well have been born a stopwatch and yet your uncle can be charming for example last year when we were walking around that park in Melilliar he didn't say anything didn't open his mouth once didn't know what to say kept looking around like he was ashamed of me but maybe he was ashamed of himself who knows at any rate I decided to do something silly to you know break the silence so I grabbed his arm and put it through mine and he looked so surprised it was incredible I mean I've never seen such big eyes they're really beautiful and that nose of his isn't bad he's got a lot going for him so don't underestimate him because if he comes with us I mean when he comes with us you'll see what he's capable of and then Mother said that I should stay calm and not worry about anything but just let it happen and not forget to shoot off the rocket once the deed was done.'

Wedding by the sea

'*Oli, oli, oli!* You know what I think, dear people? I think my little eyes have spied those rascals walking down towards the sea.'

The father, who had spoken these words to the mother, the grandmother and the grandfather, had been curled up in a long catnap ever since Lamarat had left. One by one the guests, who had spent the last two and a half days pigging out on mint tea and almonds, tore themselves away from the house and fanned out over the hillsides. (But not without taking the juiciest titbits with them: 'I'm telling you man, food galore but I didn't see hide nor hair nor bloodstained sheet of the bride and groom. "A short delay," they said. "A small hitch in the preparations," they said. If you ask me, the whole thing's a bit fishy.') One by one the platters, which had been soaking in the dishpan, were washed, rinsed and leaned against the mud walls to shine. The mother of the bride raced madly around the courtyard, trying to keep everyone from leaving. 'Aunt Latifa, why go now? Who told you, Tarir, that you shouldn't stay any longer? Besides, where else would you go this early in the evening? There's enough tea, pistachio nuts and gossip for everyone . . . more than enough. Please stay a while, in any case until we have something definite to report.' Alas and alack (for the mother) everyone left, no one stayed. In the end even the

175

flies gave up and descended on the wet tea leaves in a graceful arc to gorge themselves on the sugar.

With this deed the flies signalled the advent of evening and even the father, who was seriously beginning to wonder whether an hour consisted of sixty minutes or one, began to lose hope. 'It's just as well we're in Touarirt,' he mumbled to himself. 'The winds of scandal and shame will pass quickly over this backward, deserted peanut shell of a village. They'll ignore it, skip right over it, since even those accursed winds won't believe there are people living here.' And then, seeing as how everybody had left, nobody else was coming, and he certainly wasn't going anywhere, he looked at his father – dozing in the right corner of that long, long living room – and decided there was only one thing left to do: sleep.

When he awoke, with the horrible feeling of having slept sitting up, he heard snatches of words not meant for his ears. They seemed to be coming one by one, in a slow singsong, from behind the house. Words and an endless monologue about marbles getting stuck in someone's throat, astronauts, Roman candles, cherry bombs, exploding lumps of kohl, smurfs, making off with the money, pony camp, walking arm in arm, and just be your beautiful self. 'I'll be damned, that sounds like my daughter,' muttered the father, still half-asleep. He went into the courtyard and shook the mother and the grandmother awake. 'I heard her talking about dwarves, developmental phases – gobbledygook from middle to end. If you ask me, and I know I'm right, whatever's going on, it can't be good.'

The four of them set out, one behind the other, from big to small, like the Waltons: the father, the grandfather, the mother and the grandmother. Off they went, to the back of the house, with each of them straining their ears to hear whether any more bewitched words and sentences might still be hanging in the air.

'Drat it, son, I don't hear a thing. You must have let your dreams run away with you.'

'But-but-but, look down there . . . I saw . . . I see the three of them, down there . . . they just disappeared behind the house of that crippled old Bouchnak who was a foot soldier in Franco's army,' the grandmother cried, and she was right. 'What are we waiting for? Let's go after them.'

The mother hitched up her dress trimmed with sequins and fake crystal bells, so she could jump down to a lower terrace. 'Hurry, we've got to catch them, the devil's got into that couple. We'll bring 'em back, let 'em do what has to be done and then light out for home, away from this hellhole!'

Too stunned to say another word, the mother, the grandfather and the grandmother – where *does* she get the energy – bounded down the hillside, going down down down, terrace by terrace, step by step, weaving one by one, in single file, close on each other's heels and tangled in a bumpy conga, around the cactuses, over the rocks and down the terraces, until between their feet and the sea there was only a young man, a young woman and a victim.

'Oh, how I feel like singing a good song! Oh, how I feel like taking that man of mine, that shit-for-brains, and dunking him in the water! I'm sure you can suggest something, Ratty. Let's hear it one-two-three: *Row, row, row your boat, gently down the stream . . .*'

'. . . *merrily, merrily, merrily, merrily, life is but a dream,*' Lamarat finished for her.

As they staggered down the sandy path, the sea came closer and closer, until they were finally so close that

Rebekka said, 'Okay, this is it.' She planted a kiss on the bridegroom's lips and thrust her tongue into the slack mouth. 'I love you,' she said, 'and I always will.' When she let go, he slumped down on the sand. She staggered over to the other side of the beach, pulled up her bridal gown, squatted down, and peed. 'Don't look,' she called to Ratty, 'I'm not a film star, I'm your sister.'

Grandpa (is a sweet man) had been through a lot in his lifetime, had ploughed many fields, married off his children and wished on enough shooting stars to make all his dreams come true, but his daughter-in-law was sprinting down one tortuous trail after another with an urgency that seemed to him, at his age, to border on the obscene. Grandma, on the other hand, had no trouble keeping up the pace, since she too had been infected with the same rush of adrenaline as the woman whose umbilical cord she had once snipped in two and so skilfully poked back where it belonged. After all, female honour was at stake – it had to be captured, rescued and brought back home where it was supposed to be: between four walls. Let it escape and you'll find that the kohl has been replaced by Dior mascara, Ilikeyou lipstick and nail polish, to the shame of all those remaining within those four walls. And so the grandmother dug her heels even harder into the dirt, bounced her toes even faster off the rocks and tried, with the courage of despair, to get there before her daughter-in-law.

The father was another story. During the race down the mountain, his head was whirling with questions: *Why am I running so hard what am I doing here who else but us is going to see this spectacle those women must be mad those women are going to kill themselves on the rocks* because every time he thought he was in the lead – am I in front or are my eyes that bad? – his mother, her tongue hanging out, would practically knock him down in her hurry to get past him. 'You look like you're possessed, woman,' he snapped at her. It's a wonder, thought the father as he looked back at his father, who was hobbling a couple of feet behind him, his arms stiffly pumping the air, it's a wonder those women can move along at such a clip, what with those heavy dresses and slippers and overpowering scents – my hat's off to them.

Sis was right: she was his sister, not a peepshow in some crazy country in 'the West'. Lamarat put his hands over his face (like he did when he saw *King Kong* and *American Werewolf in London*) and pressed down on his eyeballs to keep himself from seeing a peeing sister. Exploding meteors and falling asteroids began to mass themselves, to congregate and accumulate before his eyes and make him dizzy.

From then on – when everything inside was turning to reddish bursts and everything outside to pee and pissed off – it was all a blur to Lamarat. And not just the things taking place under his nose, but also those in his head.

After she had squeezed out the last drop, Rebekka, her bridal gown bespattered, said, 'Whew, that's better,' and circled a couple of times around Mosa, whom she'd left down by the water. 'So, honeybun, what have you let yourself in for?'

Rebekka kneeled and undid his belt. 'According to the whispers I've heard tonight this young man was the darling of all the girls in Melilliar, and when I think about my future, I can only conclude that I'll be just another one of those darlings – unless of course I can rid him of this affliction.' Rebekka stopped talking, pulled a pair of scissors from under one of the layers of her dress, looked at Lamarat – who saw a silvery flash instead of scissors – and said, 'Ratty, Ratty, the moment has come to put our cards on the table: it's time you were told the true story of your birth.'

Oh, Chalid Bucket of Bolts in a Double Bed, do you hear her babbling all those secrets?

'Did you know you weren't born normally?'

'Uh, no, in what way, how exactly? I mean, what do you mean?'

'Just what I said. There isn't much to explain. That dear grandmother of yours, that motormouth who can talk faster than God can make children, took it into her head – I might as well give it to you straight – to bite your umbilical cord in half chomp-chomp instead of cutting it snip-snip in two like any clear-headed, normal person would have done.'

From then on everything got even blurrier to Lamarat. (Out of surprise at hearing what had and had not been done to him? Out of disgust at having been bitten by the hand that fed him? Or was that giant blur – the meteor crashes had made way for exploding solar systems – the result of pulling up his shirt and staring at his belly button?) Later on he never dared to talk about what had gone on, because who would believe this:

'You know what, Lamarat? Since everything is good and since everything that has been or ever will be can be recycled, Grandma has given me a brilliant idea . . . Don't you think it's fantastic that in order to save your life, I mean when it really got down to the crunch, she decided unexpectedly, on the spur of the moment, with a bit of divine prompting, to bite that hose of yours in half? Sometimes you just have to act. So to save Mosa from a life of fornifuckation with other women, I'm going to cut his hose.'

It got blurry . . . and Rebekka (her eyes bulging, her lips glistening with a greasy shine as if she'd smeared them with sheep fat, her head quivering and the rusty scissors in her right hand moving in for the kill) cut.

And the object of her undivided attention? He winced, and yawned again.

She tucked a piece of flesh – the tip of a Merquez sausage – in her cleavage and said, 'And now, my dear man and husband, it's off to the water with you, or what's left of you, so you can wash away your drunkenness along with the blood of the sacrifice.' And as Lamarat watched, she took off her clothes.

'Hey, don't look, I'm not a film star! I'm your sister.'

Lamarat quickly covered his eyes. So he didn't see her undress Mosa, didn't see her lift him up and drape him over her shoulders, didn't see Mosa and his wife, the girl who should rightfully call him 'uncle', walk into the sea. As she waded into the sparkling water, Rebekka (Lamarat could hear every word) softly sang:

> Tonight's our night,
> With punch and whoop-di-dee,
> The wedding by the sea, the wedding by the sea.
> I pledged my all to you,
> My heart and liver too,
> The wedding by the sea, the wedding by the sea.
> But you cheated and lied,
> Your love for me has died,
> It wasn't meant to be,
> The wedding by the sea, the wedding by the sea.

Together they stood in the shallow sea. Rebekka turned and tugged at her bridegroom, who had lost not only his blood, but also his honour, his strength, his everything that makes a man a man:

> The wedding by the sea, the wedding by the sea.

And they only came out of the water when the wedding night had been celebrated to her satisfaction.

When they got down to the sea, they saw Rebekka dragging Mosa towards the water and a boy standing on the sidelines with his hands over his eyes trying not to watch what was going on.

'No! Stop, don't do it Rebekka, my darling daughter, God forbid you should do it!' screamed the father, the first to arrive on the scene. 'Come out of the water and say you're all right.'

The mother, the grandfather and the grandmother, clutching their heads in dismay, were lined up behind the father.

The father looked at Lamarat and said, 'You were supposed to bring him to the house, not the sea, and you shouldn't have put him in her hands; you know as well as I do that they're not supposed to touch each other until the night of the, uh . . .'

The mother, the grandmother and the grandfather were all talking at once – it was impossible to tell who was saying what. Someone was lecturing the sea and someone else Lamarat. Anyhow, most of the words got lost in the starless, sweltering night. As foreheads were wiped, the mother gave Lamarat a tongue-lashing, 'Why didn't you go home first? And second, what are you doing here, what's she doing here, where'd all that blood come from . . . Oh, no, don't tell me it happened *here* . . . ?!'

'Oh my god!' said the father, pointing to one bloodspot after another on the sand.

He followed the trail of blood while off in a corner Rebekka helped Mosa into his clothes.

'God in heaven, that accursed wind of shame has got us after all,' the father said to his wife. 'Look, here's where he . . . and she . . . I mean this is where it happened! And he must have meant business – there's blood all over the place!'

'How will we ever be able to explain . . .'

'Shut up,' Grandpa cut in, 'and shoot off that skyrocket as fast as you can. And tomorrow . . .' He stopped for a moment and looked at his wife, '. . . tomorrow we'll play deaf, dumb and blind.'

'Oh woe is me,' Grandma moaned, completely beside herself. 'He didn't take our feelings into account, nor did he stop for a second to consider the dignity and frailty of a woman . . .'

A half-naked Rebekka came towards them, her eyes appropriately cast down.

'Don't look, don't look,' Lamarat warned. 'She's naked and she's not a film star.'

So there they were. The only thing missing was a camera, for a group portrait to hang in the house in Ollanda. On the left Lamarat with his hands over his eyes; on the right the father, the mother, the grandfather and the grandmother, looking as if water had just burst into flames; and with her back to the camera the delicate Rebekka, holding the hand of her husband – clothed in nothing more than underpants and a T-shirt – kneeling on the ground like a little boy. This is my family, thought Lamarat, and things are never going to be okay again.

Somewhere in Al Homey there's a house that's doing itself irreparable damage – glazed tiles are falling off and breaking into a thousand pieces. But the greatest damage of all has been inflicted on a male member. The tip has been cut off and, with the utmost difficulty, put back on again.

Father had carried Mosa up the mountain – with the snippet of Mosa's manhood that Rebekka had given him

('Here, it may not be too late to save it') in his left pocket – and brought him to the hospital in Al Homey, where they were puzzled by the red stain in his white jeans. 'What did they do?' the nurses whispered in the corridors. 'Deflower that idiot from behind?'

From that day forward the mother's lips were sealed. She kept her silence, like a well-known gardener once did, for six whole years, never saying a word about what had happened at the wedding by the sea. And then one Sunday afternoon she heard a friend on the other end of an international phone line: 'Mosa's never going to get better, he's flipped out completely . . . talks gibberish all day long . . . do you think it's because . . . well, you know . . . that he can't . . .'

The mother leapt up and hurled all her venom into the receiver. 'So, that monster finally got his just desserts! I always said he'd bring shame on his brother! He knew full well what he was doing, and he didn't even bother to hide it!'

After these words she never spoke of him again, and she was only really happy when he died.

Epilogue

Everyone has gone home. Lamarat went back to Ollanda with his sister. She had come through the crush zone in one piece. But since it was all too terrible for words, she preferred to keep her silence, and she kept it longer than her mother did.

The people from Iwojen didn't know exactly what had taken place, but that didn't stop them from speculating. They wondered what had happened to Mosa, what the bride had done down by the sea, how 'the kid', that strange northerner, fitted into the picture – where had he been during the scalping?

But there was one person who knew more than everyone in Iwojen put together, and that was Chalid, who said, 'I drove them to and from Melilliar. I heard all kinds of things and also thought all kinds of things that evening, but that Mosa, gosa, losa would wind up down by the sea before the day was done and that he'd crack up later on . . . well, I'm afraid I can't help you there.'

And Mosa? Not long afterwards, he sneaked off to the north, where he avoided contact with anybody who spoke his dialect and earned his living doing whatever jobs he could on the grey market. He never said a word about the loss of his thrusting power. He died insane, with a kindly smile on his face.

*

The father apparently began an interior monologue. He asked himself how it was possible for a man of his standing, a man who had built a showcase of a house, who had raised his daughter for a wedding by the sea, who had taken his brother under his wing so he could clothe him for one evening in the paraphernalia of machismo, how someone like that – the Keeper, the Embracer, the Comforter, the Alpha and the Omega – could have been hit by the ruthless, one-time winds of scandal and shame in a peanut shell of a village?

And the taxi driver – whatever happened to him? Bucket of Bolts Chalid, that freeloader and lucky devil, never played another game of Parcheesi again; he switched to a grown-up game – every Sunday he would buy one lottery ticket from ONCE, the lottery for the blind. He had a losing streak a mile wide.

But then ten years later, when Lamarat came back to visit Iwojen, he was regaled with stories of cafés that had long since been closed, winding roads that had reverted to donkey trails, a city that had satisfied its hunger for land by gobbling up the surrounding hills and gullies where little boys had once sold prickly pears to motorists (watch out for cheats) but which are now inhabited by rich, flashy, arrogant assholes who look down on games, dice and fee-fi-ho-hum-not-another-six . . . Everyone he met told him that after his village had fallen by the wayside, many more had followed: buildings are empty, houses are in ruins, people in the cities are always busy (which is more exciting, what with all those casual contacts), and in between laments they also reported: taxi driver buys a lottery ticket for the umpteenth time and BOING! – one million smakeroos! Now living in Cuba, or was it Patagonia? And just between you, me and the barstool, it seems he's started a magazine or a newspaper, 'Bucket

186

of Gold' or something like that . . . Anyway, who'd
believe it . . . it's just talk . . . though, who knows,
there may be a grain of truth in it . . . one tiny speck
of truth.